PRIMER ON
CONSTITUTIONAL LAW

PRIMER ON CONSTITUTIONAL LAW

Albert P. Melone
Southern Illinois University
at Carbondale

Carl Kalvelage
Minot State College

PALISADES PUBLISHERS
Pacific Palisades, California 90272

To Dom, Annie, Pete, and Michael

Library of Congress Catalog Card Number: 81-83775

International Standard Book Number: 0-913530-27-1

Palisades Publishers
P. O. Box 744, Pacific Palisades, California 90272-0744

Printed in the United States of America

Contents

Preface

This volume constitutes the first step in public law training. It is designed primarily for the beginning constitutional law student in need of acquiring those basic skills with legal materials necessary for getting the most from the typical undergraduate course. Upon the mastery of such basic skills, students, with the aid of instructors, will be ready to employ the modern techniques desired in a well trained student of political science.

We include such aids as how to brief a constitutional law case, an introduction to legal research, a glossary of terms, a review of the book literature, a selected bibliography, and other relevant information that has not before been available in a single volume.

The constitutional law course is a staple item in the political science curriculum. For anyone interested in understanding how values are shaped in American society, the written opinions of the Supreme Court of the United States are must reading. Students usually are required to read, brief, and analyze a great number of Supreme Court decisions. The task is not only to comprehend the legal rules and doctrines handed down by the courts, but also to appreciate the politics surrounding them and the consequences for society. On most campuses, the constitutional law course is among the most demanding. Because it often is recommended as part of a pre-law course of study, the institution's best students often enroll.

One of the unhappiest experiences encountered by both instructor and student is the poorly done undergraduate, law-related, course term paper. Not knowing any better, the student researcher will proceed as he always does, seeking out library books and popular articles. Believing that the subject has been adequately studied, the student prepares an outdated and superficial account of the topic. Because the instructor has not taken the time to discuss adequately the availability of legal research material, he or she is most reluctant to penalize the student for a poor paper. There is simply too much to cover in too little time. Usually opting to cover the substantive course material, the instructor elects not to take valuable class time to teach legal research. When a student does learn about it, it is often by trial and error, with the emphasis on the latter. We aim this text at that void.

Most of the materials found in this book have been pretested in the classroom. Given their willingness to work with the materials and to offer criticisms, the student "volunteers" have made a major contribution to this effort. Librarians, especially David Reed and Janet Syrup, gave freely of their professional talents in the early stages of this project. We express appreciation to the many public law scholars from around the country who encouraged us to seek a suitable publisher. Southern Illinois University colleagues H. B. Jacobini and Bob Roper offered particularly useful suggestions for manuscript revision. As with all her husband's projects, Peggy Melone worked in close partnership as occasional typist, as part-time reviewer and editor, and as full-time shrink. Alan Scott of Palisades Publishers and the outside reviewers, including Robert C. Welsh, University of California, Los Angeles, have carefully analyzed and exhibited enthusiasm in the project. They have made the final stages pleasant and stimulating.

Certain materials in the footnote and bibliography section of this book are based upon corresponding sections of other research texts published by General Learning Press under the pen and eye of Carl Kalvelage. We sincerely thank the publisher and the authors for their permission to use and adapt material from their texts.

Consistent with precedent, the authors share full responsibility for any errors found herein, and absolve in advance all the above named parties for any liability due to their or our own shortcomings.

A.P.M.
C.K.

PRIMER ON
CONSTITUTIONAL LAW

1

Conducting Legal Research

For the uninitiated, the prospect of using legal research material seems beyond ordinary capabilities. Even among some reference librarians we have noted an irrational fear of legal reference works. The fact is that the legal literature is among the best organized. It is designed for easy access and quick usage. In fact, private publishers compete with the frequent claim that their publications are easy to use and will save the practicing attorney valuable time. Experience teaches that once undergraduates plunge into legal materials they typically find the work not only informative but also enjoyable. Although lay people will have greater difficulty than trained attorneys, legal research material can be mastered by anyone with reasonable intelligence.

INTRODUCTION

A goal of this chapter is to provide students with an understanding of the most basic legal research tools. By no means have we attempted to provide a complete discussion of all legal research material. The tools discussed are the most fundamental but they will provide the student with the ability to do legal research for some of the most demanding undergraduate assignments. We have endeavored to present these materials free from unnecessary legal jargon and with a minimum number of assumptions about educational background. Reflecting the authors' academic interests, many examples in this chapter are from the constitutional law field. However, the materials discussed are equally applicable to a number of law-related undergraduate courses. Students of business law, criminal justice, consumer affairs, and planning law, for example, will find the presentation applicable to their studies.

Most colleges and universities will possess much of the legal research material discussed in this chapter. Those institutions with law schools will naturally provide the richest experience. For some, unfortunately, inadequate holdings will be encountered. But even this is not an insurmountable obstacle, since many community libraries have adequate law collections, and many state governments provide law libraries for public use. Investigating the alternatives can prove rewarding.

The primary source for all legal research in the United States is the reported opinions of law courts. Student textbooks typically contain edited versions of the written opinions contained in court reporter systems. Indeed all legal research material is constructed from the basic element of written judicial opinions. The reported judicial opinion is the backbone of the common law system. Without such opinions it would be impossible to cite cases as precedent and the principle of *stare decisis*—stand by past decisions—could have little meaning. With this in mind, an understanding of where opinions are located is of obvious importance.

OPINIONS OF THE UNITED STATES SUPREME COURT

Judicial opinions are published by both government and private publishing firms. This is why one often encounters more than one citation to the same case, *e.g., Dennis v. United States,* 341 U.S. 494, 95 L.Ed. 1137, 71 S.Ct. 857 (1951). Citations found in a series are often referred to as parallel citations. For the case of *Dennis* v. *United States,* three citations for the same opinion are presented. The first, 341 U.S. 494, refers to the official government publication, *United States Reports* (U.S.). The number preceding the letters U.S. (341) refers to the volume, while the number following U.S. (494) indicates the first page in volume 341 of *United States Reports* at which *Dennis* appears. The second citation (95 L.Ed. 1137) refers to the place in the *United States Supreme Court Reports—Lawyers' Edition* (L.Ed.) where the *Dennis* case may also be located; *i.e.,* Volume 95 beginning on page 1137. The *Supreme Court Reporter,* (S.Ct.), as is the *Lawyers' Edition,* is a private company publication. The citation to this set (71 S.Ct. 857) indicates that the *Dennis* case is located in Volume 71 beginning on page 857. Because students often have access to only one of the court reports it has become customary to provide the parallel citations.

All three of the court reports have one common feature. They each present the written opinions of the Supreme Court. They differ in the special features possessed by each. The *United States Reports* (U.S.) is an official report, whereas the *Lawyers' Edition* (L.Ed.) and *Supreme Court Reporter* (S.Ct.) are unofficial publications of private firms.

United States Reports (U.S.)

The first ninety volumes of this official report contain the names of the court reporter. From 1790 to 1874 the court reporter's name is on each volume and is cited, giving the reporter's name, *e.g., Marbury v. Madison,* 1 Cranch 137 (1803). But beginning in 1875 the *United States Reports* are designated by volume number, beginning with number 91 and the letters "U.S." Besides the official opinions of the Supreme Court, *United States Reports* contains summaries of facts, syllabuses, and indexes. Syllabuses (or syllabi), sometimes referred to as headnotes, are brief summaries of the important aspects of cases and contain references to the pages of the written opinions containing significant legal points.

Some time after a Supreme Court opinion is handed down, the Government Printing Office releases a "slip opinion." This opinion is its initial issue and most libraries that have *U.S. Reports* will receive them. At the end of the Court's term, the slip opinions are replaced with permanent bound volumes for that year.

United States Supreme Court Reports—Lawyers' Edition (L.Ed.)

Published by the Lawyers Co-operative Publishing Company and the Bancroft-Whitney Company, *United States Supreme Court Reports* is an outstanding private publication. It contains all Supreme Court decisions beginning with Volume 1 and has accompanying tables of parallel references to the official *United States Reports*. In addition to the opinions rendered exactly as they appear in the official reports, the *Lawyers' Edition* contains a number of features valuable to the student researcher as well as the practicing attorney. The editors prepare their own summaries of each case with headnotes (syllabuses). The appendix of each volume includes abbreviated versions of the briefs of counsel and annotations discussing important legal developments reported in the official cases. For example, the case of *Nixon v. Administrator of General Services*, 53 L.Ed. 867 (1976) gave rise to an annotation on Bills of Attainder. This 29-page essay appearing at the back of the volume is a thorough and up-to-date treatment of the topic. In short, the headnotes and annotations are most helpful to anyone interested in understanding developments in the law.

When the Supreme Court is in session, the *Lawyers' Edition* is kept current with the twice monthly publication of *Advance Sheets*. The *Advance Sheets* contain the most recent decisions of the Supreme Court with various research aids furnished by the editors. Together with other Lawyer Co-operative publications, the *Lawyers' Edition* is truly an outstanding research tool.

Supreme Court Reporter (S.Ct.)

This unofficial law reporter possesses many of the same features as the *Lawyers' Edition*. It is issued by the West Publishing Company and its headnotes and other references correlate with other West law publications. It is also supplemented with semi-monthly advance sheets when the Supreme Court is in session. The major disadvantage of the *Supreme Court Reporter* to the *Lawyers' Edition* is that it begins with Supreme Court cases since 1882. Nevertheless, as part of West's National Reporter System the *Supreme Court Reporter* is very useful.

LOWER FEDERAL COURT REPORTS

Until very recently, social scientists placed almost exclusive emphasis upon the decisions of the U.S. Supreme Court. However, there is a growing awareness that preoccupation with the high court unduly blinds us to how the judicial system really operates. Besides setting the stage for Supreme Court determination of issues, district courts and courts of appeal deal with many issues which, for one reason or another, never are decided by the highest court. These decisions may nevertheless have far reaching policy implications for the entire political system and should not be ignored. In short, much of the important activity within the judicial system takes place in the inferior federal courts and it is incumbent upon students to be aware of developments there and certainly to be familiar with this system where federal cases are reported.

Federal Cases (Fed. Cases)

Before 1880, opinions of the federal district courts and the circuit courts of appeal were scattered through a variety of law reports. This situation was remedied in 1880 when the West Publishing Company reprinted all of the previously reported federal cases in a 31-volume set named *Federal Cases*. Cases are usually reported in chronological order. However, *Federal Cases* is an exception; cases are arranged alphabetically by name of case.[1] The following is a sample citation: *United States v. Burr,* 25 Fed. Cas. 1 (No. 14, 692) (C,C, D. Kent. 1806).

Federal Reporter (Fed.)

Containing cases delivered since 1880, the *Federal Reporter,* too, is published by the West Publishing Company. Now in its second series, *Federal Reporter* contains decisions of: (1) U.S. Circuit Court (1880–1912); (2) U.S. Court of Appeals (1891–present); (3) Commerce Court of the U.S. (1911–1913), and since 1960; (4) U.S. Court of Custom of Patent Appeals (from 1943).[2] The following is a sample citation: *Penn v. San Juan Hospital, Inc.,* 528 R. 2d 1181 (10th CIR. 1975).

Federal Supplement (F. Supp.)

Also a West publication, *Federal Supplement* reports decisions of: (1) U.S. Court of Claims (1932–1960); (2) U.S. District Courts (1932–present); and (3) U.S. Custom Courts (1956–present).[3] The following is a sample citation: *Douds v. International Brotherhood, etc.* 85 F. Supp. 429 (S.D.N.Y. 1949).

---

1. J. Myron Jacobstein and Roy M. Mersky, *Fundamentals of Legal Research* (Mineola, N.Y.: The Foundation Press, Inc., 1977), p. 40.
2. *West's Law Finder: A Legal Research Manual* (St. Paul, Minn.: West Publishing Company, 1978), p. 6.
3. *Ibid.*

Federal Rules Decisions (F.R.D.)

A reporter unlikely to receive much undergraduate use, *Federal Rules Decisions* reports cases involving District Court opinions interpreting the Federal Rules of Civil and Criminal Procedure which are not reported in the *Federal Supplement.*[4] The following is a sample citation: *Tiernan v. Westext Transport, Inc.*, 46 F.R.D. 3 (1969).

STATE COURT REPORTERS

The American federal system presupposes that a large part of daily human relations will be governed by the states. Indeed, most of the nation's legal activity takes place at the state and local levels. While it is true that some federal court cases are first processed through state judicial systems, state courts are important policymaking centers independent of the federal judiciary. Some state court systems are generally perceived as trail blazers and are often cited as authority in other American courts.[5] It is apparent, then, that state court decisions should not be ignored. A working knowledge of state court reporters is a necessary prerequisite for comprehending policymaking in the entire judicial system.

About three-fourths of the states publish their own official court reports. Some have elected to report only opinions of the highest state court. Others report all appellate courts and some publish only decisions of trial courts.[6] As part of its National Reporter System, the West Publishing Company has made available state appellate decisions for all the states and trial court opinions for some states. The West Company has divided the nation into seven geographical regions. The *North Western Reporter* was the first to be published beginning in 1879. On the following page is a listing of each regional reporter describing the states covered with a sample citation for each.

Probably reflecting case volume and market considerations, the West Company also publishes two specific reporters. First released in 1887, the *New York Supplement* reports all opinions of the New York Court of Appeals, all decisions of the Appellate Division of the Supreme Court, and all opinions of the lower courts of record. In 1960, the *California Reporter* made its debut. It reports all decisions of the California Supreme Court, the California District Courts of Appeal, and the California Supreme Court, Appellate Department.

The most recent addition to the reporter system is the *Military Justice Reporter.* It contains decisions of the United States Court of Military Appeals

---

4. *Ibid.*, pp. 6–7.

5. For a general discussion of state courts see: Kenneth N. Vines and Herbert Jacob, "Public Policy in the States," in Herbert Jacob and Kenneth N. Vines, ed. *Politics in the American States: A Comparative Analysis,* (Boston: Little, Brown and Company, 1976), pp. 242–266. The classic article on the influence of state courts is: Rodney Mott, "Judicial Influence," 30 *American Political Science Review*, pp. 295–315 (April, 1936).

6. Jacobstein, *Fundamentals of Legal Research*, pp 54–57.

Reporter	States Covered and Sample Citation
North Western Reporter 1879–1940 (1st series) 1940–present (2nd series)	Iowa, Michigan, Minnesota, Nebraska, North Dakota, South Dakota, Wisconsin. *General Homes, Inc. v.* *Tower Insurance Co.*, 67 Wis. 2d 97, 226 N.W. 2nd 394 (1975).
Pacific Reporter 1883–1931 (1st series) 1931–present (2nd series)	Alaska, Arizona, California, Colorado, Hawaii, Idaho, Kansas, Montana, Nevada, New Mexico, Oklahoma, Oregon, Utah, Washington, Wyoming. *Byrd et. al. v.* *Peterson et. al.*, 66 Ariz. 253, 186 p. 2d 955 (1947).
Atlantic Reporter 1885–1938 (1st series) 1938–present (2nd series)	Connecticut, Delaware, Maine, Maryland, New Hamp- shire, New Jersey, Pennsylvania, Rhode Island, Vermont, and District of Columbia Municipal Court of Appeals. *Adams v. Barrell,* 132 A. 130 (Me. 1926).
North Eastern Reporter 1885–1936 (1st series) 1936–present (2d series)	Illinois, Indiana, Massachusetts, New York, Ohio. *People v. Savino,* 44 N.Y. 2d 669, 376 N.E. 2d 196 (1978).
South Eastern Reporter 1887–1939 (1st series) 1939–present (2d series)	Georgia, North Carolina, South Carolina, Virginia, West Virginia. *Greer v. Greer,* 128 S.E. 2d 51 (Ga. 1962).
Southern Reporter 1887–1940 (1st series) 1940–present (2d series)	Alabama, Florida, Louisiana, Mississippi. *Long v.* *Woollard,* 163 So. 2d 698 (Miss. 1964).
South Western Reporter 1886–1940 (1st series) 1940–present (2d series)	Arkansas, Kentucky, Missouri, Tennessee, Texas, Indian Territory. *Hunt v. State,* 48 S.W. 2d 466 (Tx. 1932).

and the Army, Navy, Air Force, and Coast Guard Courts of Military Review.

All West law publications contain a number of attractive reference features not found in official reports published by government. The most important feature, to be discussed later in this chapter under the Digest topic, is the West Key Number System. The important point to note is that all West publications are coordinated in a way that provides the researcher with an interlocking research network. Mastering West's system is not as difficult as one might surmise; the payoffs are worth the effort.

AMERICAN LAW REPORTS (A.L.R.)

The *American Law Reports* does not fit neatly into the category of a court reporter. Although it reports judicial opinions, its primary function extends beyond this. The *A.L.R.* series is best employed as an excellent annotation elaborating upon important judicial opinions.

A Lawyers Co-operative and Bancroft-Whitney publication, the *American Law Reports* is a highly selective case reporter. The editors choose for inclusion those cases they feel are of general legal significance—cases that illustrate important legal developments. Following the judicial opinion, an impartial treatment of the law relevant to the particular case is provided. Each annotation is a detailed treatise on the specific legal topic. The annotation discusses in great detail the inception, development and contemporary applicability of the law relating to the reported judicial opinions.[7] As such, *A.L.R.* is an excellent study guide for anyone interested in specific legal topics.

First published in 1919, *A.L.R.* is now in its fourth series. *A.L.R. 1st* covers the period 1919 to 1948 and contains 175 volumes. *A.L.R. 2nd* deals with legal topics for 1948 to 1965 and appears in 100 volumes. *A.L.R. 3rd* contains both state and federal topics from 1965 to 1969 and since 1969 deals only with state law topics. *A.L.R. Federal* reports only federal law topics commencing in 1969.[8]

A.L.R. is accompanied by several relatively easy to use indexes. The *A.L.R.* series is especially useful when employed in conjunction with other Lawyer Co-operative publications. It contains references to other Lawyer Co-operative publications which in turn contain references to it.

Without disparaging the *A.L.R.* series, for those student researchers interested in locating a large body of cases the West National Reporter System is probably the superior tool. The Lawyers Co-operative editors provide an excellent treatment for relatively fewer cases while the West Company has elected to provide more cases without the very elaborate editorial annotations.

ADMINISTRATIVE AGENCY REPORTING

Fulfilling many of the same functions as law courts and in many instances having a similar impact upon citizens and institutions, administrative agencies are vitally important to understanding legal processes. Administrative rules and regulations do not appear in court reporters. However, these materials are easily accessible and are published by the U.S. government in two specialized publications, the *Federal Register* and the *Code of Federal Regulation*.

Federal Register

Since 1936 all federal administrative rules and regulations are published in the *Federal Register*.[9] The *Register* is published daily and all materials are arranged chronologically. It contains newly adopted rules and regulations, notice of proposed regulations and rules, dates of administrative hearings, and decisions of administrative bodies. It also contains presidential executive orders and proclamations and is indexed monthly, quarterly, and annually.

7. *The Living Law: A Guide to Legal Research Through the Pages of a Modern System* (The Lawyers Co-operative Publishing Company, Bancroft-Whitney Company, 1978), p. 23.

8. Ibid., p. 24.

9. For a history and full explanation of the Federal Register system see: National Archives and Records Service, General Services Administration, *The Federal Register: What it is and How to Use it* (Washington, D.C.: Government Printing Office, 1977).

Code of Federal Regulations (C.F.R.)

Because the *Federal Register* is arranged chronologically and not by subject, it is practically impossible to use it when attempting to ascertain rules and regulations by subject matter or agency. The *Register* must be used in conjunction with the *Code of Federal Regulations*. The C.F.R. is arranged under fifty separate titles and is published in pamphlet form on an annual basis. Because C.F.R. is revised each year, the researcher is in a position to begin to discern which rules and regulations are currently in force. It contains an easy to use annual index accompanied by monthly updates.

When attempting to update rules and regulations the researcher should use the *Code of Federal Regulations* together with the daily *Federal Register*. After consulting the annual index to C.F.R., the researcher should then consult the monthly cumulative issue entitled, *LSA: List of CFR Sections Affected*. This procedure will give the researcher an up-to-date account for the year and month. However, rules and regulations are changed and promulgated on a daily basis, so it is necessary to find the latest possible changes. This goal can be achieved by turning to the most recent daily *Federal Register*. Each *Register* contains a section titled, "Cumulative List of Parts Affected." Utilizing this research procedure will yield a complete and current understanding of agency rules and regulations.

LEGAL ENCYCLOPEDIAS

Encyclopedias are elementary research tools commonly employed by students in elementary school through college. Yet most students are unaware that legal encyclopedias are available and represent a convenient research tool for any one interested in legal questions.

Legal encyclopedias are of three varieties: general, local, and specialized. For undergraduate purposes, the general encyclopedias are most useful. Encyclopedias dealing with local law and special subjects are of particular interest to the legal practitioner. Local law encyclopedias cover case and statutory law of a specific state. Fewer than a third of the states have them. Special subject encyclopedias contain fairly comprehensive discussions of specific legal topics, for example, automobiles, private corporations, or evidence.

The two general encyclopedias commonly held by libraries are *American Jurisprudence 2d (Am. Jur. 2d)* and *Corpus Juris Secundum (C.J.S.)*. American Jurisprudence 2d replaces *American Jurisprudence,* and *Corpus Juris Secundum* likewise supersedes the old *Corpus Juris*. Both *Am. Jur. 2d* and *C.J.S.* are publications of private companies which employ legal experts to write on various topics. They are not official government documents.

The encyclopedias contain articles on specific legal topics. These articles differ from a legal treatise or an article in a legal periodical in that there is no overt attempt to argue the merits of particular legal rules or principles. Rather, the writers attempt to present clear, concise, and objective statements on the law of a particular topic. Both *Am. Jur. 2d* and *C.J.S.* are excellent tools for beginning research into a legal question. Besides an exposition on the law, the topical discussions are accompanied with cross-references to other legal research materials including, for example, cases, digests, statutory provisions, and annotations. Students will often desire to go from the encyclopedia exposition to the other cited sources for a more detailed understanding of the subject-matter.

American Jurisprudence 2d

Am. Jur. 2d is a discussion of both substantive and procedural aspects of American law arranged in more than 400 title headings. This particular encyclopedia places great emphasis upon federal statutory law and federal procedural rules. Students interested in detailed reference to state laws will be disappointed, although *Am. Jur. 2d* makes extensive references to the *Uniform State Laws*.

The volumes are arranged alphabetically by title. For those already familiar with a particular legal topic, one might go directly to the titled volume. Preceding the exposition of each legal topic is an abstract and outline of the subject. By reading the brief abstract and perusing the subject outline, the researcher can easily determine if he or she has turned to the appropriate discussion. This method, however, presupposes a sophistication probably lacking in most undergraduate students. It is preferable to refer to the *General Index* for locating the subject matter of interest.

The simple procedures for using the *General Index* can be illustrated by an example. Assume that a student researcher is interested in investigating housing discrimination for a course in civil rights. Perhaps the first topic which comes to mind is civil rights. In this case, the researcher's view of the topic is rather broad. Turning to the index item, "Civil Rights," appearing in Volume C of the *General Index,* he finds on page 276 the entry: "Housing Laws and Urban Redevelopment (this index)." The researcher then knows that the topic of housing discrimination is most likely contained under "Housing Laws and Urban Redevelopment," and turning to this index item, he or she will find his topic. Of course, he could have avoided the wasted motion by thinking more carefully about the subject before beginning to search the index. If he had focused immediately upon the subject, housing discrimination, he would have turned to the General Index, volume F-I. On page 855 of this particular index is located the entry: "Housing Laws and Urban Redevelopment," with the subheading entry, "discrimination." One will also find a subheading termed, "generally, . . ." Immediately below this entry are 34 additional subheadings. Whether the researcher begins the search with a broad or a specific subject category in mind, one should recognize that there is no need to despair because the Index is cross-referenced for easy access to the substantive discussions of law.

Having located the correct subject entry in the *Index,* a person's next step is to turn from the *Index* to the appropriate volume of *Am. Jur. 2d.* For the case of housing discrimination, one will note that a general discussion is found under Civ R § § 249–256. Most will immediately realize that the abbreviation Civ R refers to Civil Rights. But for the more difficult or uncommon abbreviations one need only consult the "Table of Abbreviations" appearing at the front of each copy of the *General Index.* The symbol refers to the subsection under Civil Rights where the discussion of the topic will be found. Thus volume 15 of *Am. Jur. 2d* contains materials ranging in alphabetical order from Charities to Civil Rights. Turning to §§ 249–256 under Civil Rights we find a discussion of housing discrimination, beginning on page 775 and ending on page 797.

The exposition on the law contains extensive references to original source material such as statutes, executive orders, and case law. Secondary sources are also cited including annotations to the *American Law Reports. American Jurisprudence 2d* thus provides an excellent starting point for researching a legal subject. Although it is very useful in obtaining a general overview of the law on a particular subject, the student will probably want to consult additional research materials often cited in this encyclopedia.

Corpus Juris Secundum (C.J.S.)

Like *Am. Jur. 2d, Corpus Juris Secundum (C.J.S.)* is a massive statement of U.S. case law. It consists of 101 volumes with over 400 separate titles and a five volume *General Index.* This impressive encyclopedia includes references to reported cases decided as long ago as the mid-seventeenth century. It contains extensive references to state as well as federal law. Each subject essay is updated with an annual pocket supplement found in the back of each bound volume. Whole volumes are occasionally replaced with totally updated versions.

Written primarily for practicing attorneys, the publisher (West Publishing Company) has devised time-saving methods for finding the law on any given subject.[10] For the most part, the use of these methods presupposes a general knowledge of law not possessed by the undergraduate. Yet by employing similar elementary techniques as were described for *Am. Jur. 2d,* anyone can successfully use *C.J.S.*

A simple way to proceed is first to consult the five-volume *General Index* where, as one might expect, topics are listed in alphabetical order. By beginning with the most general title and then proceeding to locate the most specific sub-title, the student can quickly focus on a particular subject. However, the *General Index* is designed to be used in close conjunction with the title indexes to each *C.J.S.* subject matter title. Therefore, before turning to the specific subject essay, it is advisable to examine carefully the *Analysis* which

---

10. For a discussion of these methods see: *West's Law Finder: A Research Manual for Lawyers* (St. Paul, Minn.: West Publishing Company, 1967).

appears at the beginning of each subject title. Thus the student-researcher should consult the appropriate volume of the encyclopedia itself for a detailed description of the subject matter discussion contained therein.

The *Analysis* briefly describes the nature of the topic and provides an outline of the general topic in its related parts. This time-saving procedure will provide the student with both an overview of the subject matter and how the specific topic fits into the general legal framework. In addition to legal essays, each volume contains its own index. Moreover, at the back of each volume is an index to words, phrases, and legal maxims found there—a feature providing dictionary-type definitions.

A brief example illustrates the research procedure. Let us say that in a course on the criminal justice system the question of whether prison officials may search inmate mail comes up. Because no one knows the answer to the question, your instructor asks you to investigate and report your findings to the class at its next meeting.

Turning to the *General Index M–Q,* you find "Prisons" beginning on page 777 and ending on page 783. Since there are numerous subheadings, it is necessary to narrow your investigation further. On page 782 you find: "Searches and seizures, prisoners' mail, Searches § 30." Having successfully narrowed the index search to the desired topic you turn from the *Index* to the appropriate subject matter volume. Since "Searches" falls alphabetically within Volume 79—"Schools, etc. 323 to End—Sessions," you find Searches 30 located on page 798. Directly under the title heading, in bold print, you first locate a brief statement on the general rule of law. A paragraph follows explaining applications of the rule with citations to a number of state and federal cases. You have also taken the time to consult the *Analysis* under Searches and Seizures and are in a position to discuss searches of prisoners' mail within the general context of search and seizure law.

CODES

A code is a systematic compilation of statutory law. It is often accompanied by annotations to judicial decisions interpreting the legislative enactments. Legislative bodies codify law in order to make the statutory law consistent in its various parts and thereby avoid duplication and ambiguity. For the citizen, codification permits each person access to the law of particular subjects in a quick and efficient fashion. Codes are a valuable tool for students interested in public law; the annotated codes, in particular, are useful because they contain illuminating histories and interpretations.

In the United States there are federal, state and municipal codes. Most codes contain texts of statutes, constitutions, legislative histories, annotations to judicial decisions, various tables, and useful indexes. Although state and municipal codes are useful, they are analogous in form to the various federal codes, and need not be discussed here. Only codes dealing with federal law will be considered.

Currently there are three widely available federal codes: The *United States Code, 1976 Edition (U.S.C.)* as supplemented by the *1979 Supplement* is the official statement of the law. The *United States Code Annotated (U.S.C.A.)* and the *United States Code Service (U.S.C.S.)* are produced by private companies but possess features not available in the official *United States Code.*

United States Code (U.S.C.)

Congress has arranged U.S. codified law under 50 separate titles. These titles include, for example: Title 3, the President; Title 10, Armed Forces; and Title 43, Public Lands. The titles are further subdivided into subtitles, parts, chapters, subchapters, and sections. The four-part *General Index* is extensive, permitting the researcher to find the law relatively quickly. Unfortunately the *United States Code* is of limited use since it does not contain many features found in the unofficial codes.

United States Code Service (U.S.C.S.)

The *United States Code Service* is a remarkably useful research tool. Among its many features are the exact language from the *Statutes at Large,* legislative histories, annotations of interpretative case law, reference to relevant law review articles, an excellent five-volume *General Index,* and individual title indexes. This set also contains an excellent two-volume annotation of the U.S. Constitution. The entire set is kept current through supplements inserted at the back of each appropriate volume.

The *United States Code Service* is the successor to the *Federal Code Annotated (F.C.A.).* In fact, the *U.S.C.S.* volumes are signified by blue labels on black bindings, while the parent *F.C.A.* volumes are easily recognized with their red labels on similar black bindings. As the *F.C.A.* volumes are superseded by *U.S.C.S.* editions, the entire set will have blue labels on black bindings.

The editors of *U.S.C.S.* have arranged the code in the same way as the official *U.S.C.* For example, the codification of law dealing with commerce and trade can be found in both the official *U.S.C.* and the unofficial *U.S.C.S.* under Title 15. Most students will not be sufficiently familiar with the various official titles to turn directly to the code when commencing research. For this reason, on most occasions the researcher is best advised to consult the five-volume *General Index.* If, however, the researcher knows the popular name of a law, for example, the Taft-Hartley Act, he or she should consult the special volume index containing popular names.

What makes *U.S.C.S.* particularly useful are the extensive research aids. It has, of course, the complete text of the relevant law. It makes references to amendments and contains a complete research guide. For example, it points out where in the legal encyclopedia, *American Jurisprudence 2d,* a related discussion is found. Its numerous annotations discuss how the law has been construed by judicial bodies. A very attractive feature is its bibliographic reference to law review articles on the various topics.

For students of constitutional law, the two volumes containing the Constitution's Articles and Amendments provide an extensive research guide. These volumes contain many of the research aids included in the Code. Under the Fourth Amendment, for instance, one finds the exact wording of the constitutional provision, cross references, a research guide, annotated references to court cases, and statutory law. Relevant law review articles and interpretative notes are also provided. Students assigned the task of writing a paper on a particular constitutional provision will find this feature of *U.S.C.S.* valuable.

United States Code Annotated (U.S.C.A.)

Better known and more widely used than *U.S.C.S.*, the *United States Code Annotated (U.S.C.A.)* is published by the West Publishing Company. It also annotates relevant judicial interpretations and features collateral references to the many other West publications. This fine set contains an eight-volume index and a multiple volume treatment of each provision of the U.S. Constitution. As with *U.S.C.S.*, consulting the *General Index* or *Popular Name Index* is the best way to research a statutory topic.

Students interested in bringing their research up to date are advised to consult the pocket supplements of each volume. One should also proceed to the *Supplementary Pamphlet* when one is published. And finally, always consult the last published pamphlet of the *U.S. Code Congressional and Administrative News*. It cumulates the changes in the statute since the publications of the *U.S.C.A.* pocket supplements and the latest *Supplementary Pamphlet*.

DIGESTS

The lay person is often impressed when he hears an attorney rattle off a number of precedents in support of his client's claim. It is thought that the attorney has done his homework and must have put in many long and arduous hours locating all those cases. Although it is probably true that the attorney did his homework, the time devoted to the research is not as long as one might suppose. A digest is an available research tool designed to find cases on a particular legal topic without reading all the reported cases in American law. The lawyer's need for such a device is obvious. Yet identifying all relevant cases on a particular legal subject is also a useful exercise for undergraduates. Students are often asked to write term papers that explore the shape of U.S. law in a particular subject area. The ability to use a digest can facilitate the research process and lead to an up-to-date presentation.

Fundamentally, digests are necessary because of the way court decisions are reported. Cases are reported chronologically, not according to topic or subject. A digest is an index to the reported cases according to subject matter, providing brief abstracts of the facts or holdings in a case. Unlike an encyclopedia, a digest does not present a narrative on the law with accompanying footnotes. Simply put, a digest is a research tool that seeks out the cases dealing with particular facts or legal problems. Since the digest is only an index, it is always necessary to proceed to the actual court decisions for reading and analyses.

Digests are published to accommodate a variety of needs. A national digest is available if a researcher is interested in all reported U.S. cases. If he or she is interested only in a particular part of the country, regional digests are published. Digests are also available for a number of state jurisdictions. And lastly, digests are published covering particular court systems. We will describe the digest system for all American law and for the more specialized court systems. The regional and state digests are segments of the national digest and are used by researchers in the same way.

American Digest System

The *American Digest System* is a colossal work consisting of over 327 volumes. It is a subject classification of all reported cases appearing in the *National Reporter System*. The first set of this digest system, known as the *Century Digest*, covers the period from 1685 to 1896. For each succeeding ten-year period there are decennial digests from the *First Decennial* (1897–1906) to the *Eighth Decennial* (1966–1976). For the period since 1976 the *General Digest* is available, supplemented by monthly issues which are eventually bound. All the abstracted cases are arranged according to the West Publishing Company, "Key Number System."

Key Number System. The "Key Number System" is West's scheme for assigning cases or sections of cases to appropriate subject categories. This system first divides the law into seven main classes. Each class is then divided into subclasses and then each subclass is divided into topics. The topics are further divided into subdivisions. Finally, a Key Number is assigned to each subdivision.[11] By first identifying the appropriate topic and key number, the researcher can locate all reported cases on a particular topic. In other words, by going through each *Decennial* and *General Digest* it is possible to identify all the cases on a given topic. Although there are more aids, two methods of using the Key Number System are best suited for undergraduate use, *Table of Cases Index* and the *Descriptive-Word Index*.

Employing the *Table of Cases Index* can best be illustrated by way of example. After reading the Supreme Court's decision in *Griswold* v. *Connecticut* (1965), the student becomes interested in the right to privacy topic.

11. *West's Law Finder: A Research Manual for Lawyers* (St. Paul, Minn.: West Publishing Company, 1978), pp. 16–20; Also see: Jacobstein and Merskey, *Fundamentals of Legal Research*, pp. 66–72.

Among other things, he or she is interested in identifying all the cases dealing with the constitutional protection of privacy. Each *Decennial* and *General Digest* contains an alphabetical listing of cases by plaintiff, in our example, Griswold. Since *Griswold* v. *Connecticut* was decided in 1965, the *Table of Cases Index* for the *Seventh Decennial* is employed. By looking up *Griswold* v. *Connecticut* the student finds its legal citation and the various Topic and Key Numbers under which the case has been digested. After deciding upon the appropriate Topic and Key Number, the student need only consult each *Decennial* and *General Digest* for a complete abstract of all reported cases under the selected Topic and Key Number.

Using the *Descriptive-Word Index* is a second and sometimes quicker method for locating Topics and Key Numbers. While this method is less time consuming than the case index approach, it requires more thought. There is a separate *Descriptive-Word Index* to each unit of the *Decennials* and *General Digest*. By thinking of a "magic word," or catch word, the student may consult this index to determine whether there is such an entry. For our example, "privacy" is an obvious magic word for cases involving the doctrine found in *Griswold* v. *Connecticut*. In most cases, however, selecting the right word will prove more difficult. But since there are hundreds of word entries, the student researcher does not need to despair after failing the first attempt. Try additional "magic words" and soon the desired reference will be found.

It must be reemphasized that the West Publishing Company has devised a variety of ways to find the desired cases. But their methods were created for those who have had legal training, not undergraduate students. We recommend, therefore, that the student employ the table of cases and the descriptive word indexes because these tools require little in terms of advanced legal training. While the Key Number System may seem difficult to comprehend at first, working with the material will build confidence.

Specialized Digests

It was previously indicated that the West Publishing Company also publishes a number of regional, state and federal digests.[12] It is important to note that each of these more specialized digests is a segment of the *American Digest System*. As a consequence, if one has access to the parent *American Digest System*, he really has no great need to consult the more specialized digests. Sometimes, reflecting academic interests, college or university libraries will be in possession of one or more of the specialized digests and not the more extensive *American Digest System*. Students of constitutional law will find the *Federal Practice Digest, 2d* and the *U.S. Supreme Court Digest* well suited for most research purposes.

12. The regional digests correspond to the regional reporter system of the West Publishing Company. The regional digests are: *Atlantic Digest, North Western Digest, Pacific Digest, South Eastern Digest* and *Southern Digest*. Some include second series digests.

Federal Practice Digest, 2d. If the researcher's topic includes only federal case law, the *Federal Practice Digest, 2d* is the digest to use. Because it, too, is a West Publishing Company publication, the West Key-Number System is employed. Since it includes all reported federal cases including, for example, federal district courts, courts of appeal, and the U.S. Supreme Court decisions, *Federal Practice Digest, 2d* is a valuable aid to anyone interested in understanding the corpus juris of the entire federal judicial system. Its special features include paragraphs indicating whether a case has been affirmed, reversed, or modified as well as references to secondary sources such as *Corpus Juris Secundum.*

Federal Practice Digest, 2d indexes cases since 1961. For earlier cases (1939–1961) one must consult *Modern Federal Practice Digest* and for still earlier cases the *Federal Digest* should be used. The set is kept current by annual pocket supplements and subsequent pamphlet supplements.

U.S. Supreme Court Digest (West Publishing Company). The *U.S. Supreme Court Digest* contains only digests of decisions of the U.S. Supreme Court. It also utilizes the Key Number System and duplicates the cases found in the *American Digest System* and the *Federal Practice Digest, 2d* series. It, too, is kept up to date by cumulative annual packet supplements. This 17-volume digest is ideal for research projects requiring only U.S. Supreme Court decisions.

U.S. Supreme Court Reports Digest: Lawyers' Edition. This Supreme Court digest is published by the Lawyers Co-operative Publishing Company, the same firm that issues *American Jurisprudence, 2d* and *United States Code Service.* Since it is not a West publication it does not employ the Key-Number System. The *U.S. Supreme Court Reports Digest* is easy to use and contains both a *Table of Cases* and a *Word Index.*

The *Table of Cases* lists U.S. Supreme Court decisions under both plaintiff and defendant names. It also presents the popular names under which cases are sometimes known. Below the alphabetical listing for each case, the full case citation is given, followed by the topic and section number(s) under which each case is digested. Rather than proceeding directly to the digest topic and number designation, it is advisable to consult first the scope-note and outline preceding each topic title. The scope-notes define the nature of each topic. This enables the researcher to determine whether the correct topic has been chosen. For example, the case of *Abrams* v. *U.S.* is digested under four different topics, *i.e.,* Appeal and Error, Constitutional Law, Criminal Law, and Evidence. As is common for all digests, the editors abstract cases under a number of different topics. Choosing the topic title of greatest research interest can be achieved by consulting the scope-notes and outlines before reading each of the digest entries. By doing so, the researcher can save time and considerable effort.

The *Word Index* to *U.S. Supreme Court Reports Digest: Lawyers' Edition* is utilized in the same way as West's *Descriptive Word Index*. Simply attempt to think of those "magic words" which best describe the relevant subject matter. If at first you do not succeed, try again and again. There are thousands of words from which to choose. After some practice, you will find this method preferable to the *Table of Cases* approach.

In addition to the abstracts of each Supreme Court case, the editors have included references to the *Am. Jur.* series and to annotations relevant to the case. As a consequence, this fine digest can be used easily in conjunction with other Lawyer Co-operative publications.

Volume 17 of this 20-volume set contains a couple of features particularly valuable to consitutional law students. First, each Article, Section, and Clause of the Constitution appears with digest references. For example, under Article I, Section 8, Clause 3 (the commerce clause), the digest reference: Commerce §§ 1–360 is given. Thus all Supreme Court cases dealing with the commerce clause can be readily located.

A second useful feature of this volume is the inclusion of the *Revised Rules of the Supreme Court of the United States*. Such common questions as what constitutes a quorum for the Court, or what are the rules governing the granting of certiorari can be answered. This *Rules* section also includes a research guide with references to the *Supreme Court Reports Digest* and *American Jurisprudence, 2d*.

As with most legal research material, the *Supreme Court Reports Digest: Lawyers' Edition* is kept current by pocket supplements inserted at the back of each bound volume. The supplements should always be consulted.

CITATORS

A citator is an additional tool with which to find the law. It differs from a digest in several ways: It is not arranged according to subject matter; it does not provide written abstracts of cases; and its principal function is different. A citator is designed to determine quickly how cited cases have been treated by subsequent court decisions. For example, has a particular case been sustained, overruled, or perhaps modified by a later court decision? Thus it is possible to ascertain the current status of a rule of law determined many years ago.

The attorney needs a citator for an obvious reason. It would certainly be an embarrassment to argue a case on the basis of a precedent that has long been overruled. The attorney would probably lose the case. For the undergraduate, a citator is a valuable device to assure that a court decision is now currently in force. For example, if after reading *Minersville School District v. Gobitis* 310 U.S. 586 (1940) the student concludes that compulsory flag salutes are constitutionally permissible, he would surely be wrong. The fact is that in *West Virginia State Board of Education v. Barnette* 319 U.S. 624 (1943) the

Supreme Court overruled *Gobitis.* Using a citator would have prevented this gross error.

Citators are available for a number of different jurisdictions and subjects. All the citators are published by Shepard's Citations, Inc., now a division of McGraw-Hill. Just a few uses of citators are: U.S. Supreme Court cases; lower federal courts; state cases; criminal justice; federal labor law; U.S. Constitution; federal statutes; and law reviews. To illustrate the use of citators, the Shepard's citator for the U.S. Supreme Court will be described.

Shepard's United States Citations: Cases

Upon opening the maroon colored cover of one of the huge volumes in this set, the initial reaction typically is frustration. What seems to be an immense blur of tiny legal citations placed on very thin pages hits us with a wallop. One's first reaction is to put the volume quietly back on the shelf and to forget the whole idea. But wait! Like most legal research material, the citator is easy to use.

The starting point in using the citator is a legal citation to a court case. You want to locate those cases that cite your case in a significant fashion. Because sometimes a researcher has a citation for only one of the reporting systems, the Shepard editors have separate sections of each volume reserved for each of the three parallel citations for each case: *United States Reports* (U.S.); the unofficial *Lawyer's Edition* (L.Ed.); or West's unofficial *Supreme Court Reporter* (S.Ct.). Beginning with a citation to a particular case (for example, 310 U.S. 586), one locates the volume number of the citation (310) at the upper corner of each printed page of the citator. Because the volume numbers are arranged numerically, this is an easy task. On the body of each page, printed in bold numerals, is the page number of each case, in our example (586). Once the desired case has been located by volume and page number, the task of locating the citing cases may begin.

Because the editors have included a case citation whenever a judge cites a case in his written opinion, the number of citations is often great. The result of this editorial decision is to list a citing case whenever a judge mentions a cited case, even vaguely or incorrectly. Obviously reading each one of these citing cases would be an unnecessary and enormous task. To circumvent this obvious difficulty, the editors have provided cues whenever a cited case has been treated in a significant manner; for example, when a case is distinguished or overruled. These cues are presented in the form of lower case letters appearing at the left edge of the cited or citing cases. These lower case letters are abbreviations for explanations of how the case was cited.

A complete listing of these abbreviations and definitions is provided in each volume. By running one's finger down the left edge of the columns, the cues can be noted. To determine the context and language utilized by the court in its decision, the researcher should then read the citing case in either the official or unofficial reports.

The compulsory flag salute cases provide a relatively uncomplicated example to illustrate the use of this citator. The research problem is to determine the rule of law with respect to the flag salute question. Armed with the *Gobitis* decision, the research begins. The official citation for *Minersville School District* v. *Gobitis* is 310 U.S. 586; 310 refers to volume 310 of the *United States Reports* (U.S.), 586 directs one to the first page in volume 310 in which *Gobitis* appears. We note that Volume IB of *Shepard's United States Citations* contains citations for Supreme Court cases reported in volumes 151–313 of *United States Reports*. Because the cases are arranged in numerical order, we skip the pages to find 310. On page 3203 of *Citations* we locate 310 U.S. 586.

Under 586 we first locate the parallel citations to the *Lawyer's Edition* (L.Ed.) and West's *Supreme Court Reporter* (S.Ct.). Immediately below these citations are several cites to cases describing the judicial history of the *Gobitis* case in the federal courts. At the left of these cites are the editor's cue in the form of the lower case s. The s indicates that the federal court case has been superseded by the Supreme Court decision being cited.

This sequence of entries is followed by a heading titled: Const. Law, Freedom of Religion. This in turn is followed by a citation to a lower federal court decision which cited *Gobitis*. After this single citation is the appearance of another entry heading: School Regulations—Mandatory Flag Salute. This heading is followed by a number of federal and state cases also citing *Gobitis*.

Because the researcher is interested only in the issue of compulsory flag salute, the cases appearing under this last heading are especially relevant. But the editors have not provided special cues in the form of special notations. Unless the researcher is interested in describing cases in which the *Gobitis* decision has been mentioned, this series of citations is of little value. The problem is to determine whether the holding in *Gobitis* remains the rule of law.

Since *Shepard's Volume IB* contains cases up to the year 1943, it is necessary to consult additional volumes and supplements to the current year. Turning to the *1943–1971 Supplement*, we find on page 888 additional citations to *Gobitis*. Quickly we find an entry for 319 U.S. 642 with a cue in the form of a lower case o. The notation o means that 310 U.S. 586 (*Gobitis*) has been overruled by 319 U.S. 642 (*West Virginia State Board of Education* v. *Barnette*.)[13] Following the *Barnette* entry are numerous citations to federal and state cases which cite *Gobitis* in some way.

Up to this point we have discovered that the Shepard's editors indicate that *Gobitis* has been overruled by *Barnette*. To verify the editor's assessment

---

13. The reader will note that the page number citation for *Barnette* differs from the one presented earlier. The reason is that the Shepard's editors provide the exact page within the *Barnette* opinion where the *Gobitis* case is directly overruled.

and to determine the precise reasoning of the court, we should turn to the actual case for reading and analysis. But having done this, we are not prepared to report that *Barnette* is the existing rule of law. Once again we must turn to the citator, repeating the research procedure this time for the *Barnette* case. In Volume 3 of *Shepard's United States Citations—Cases,* we locate on page 95 the citation for 319 U.S. 642. There are numerous entries of decisions citing *Barnette,* but no cue or notation indicating that *Barnette* has been overruled. Consulting the later supplements indicates likewise.

Shepard's United States Citations: Statutes

The *Statutes* edition of *Shepard's United States Citations* contains citations to: U.S. Constitution; *United States Code; United States Code Annotated; Federal Code Annotated; United States Statutes at Large; United States Treaties and other International Agreements; General Orders in Bankruptcy;* and court rules for a number of courts including the U.S. Supreme Court.

This two-volume set with supplements contains a variety of references including citations to court decisions. If, for example, one is interested in knowing how the courts have construed the Eleventh Amendment, this citator provides a listing of cases citing the Amendment. The same is true for the codes and other special features of this citator. One should consult the preface and other explanatory remarks provided at the beginning of these volumes for discussion and illustrations of its contents.

LEGAL PERIODICALS

Law periodicals can be read from at least three perspectives. First, law review or journal material is a secondary source for what the law has been, what it is at any given moment, and what it might become. Second, law articles reflect conflicting expert opinion concerning what the law should become. And third, law articles can teach students of the judiciary about the more subtle attempts to influence the bench and bar.

Law articles, commonly, are well documented and meticulous discussions on a variety of legal or law-related topics. These articles are an excellent source. They provide the student with the history of the law and its more recent developments. A common student error, however, is to treat these articles, no matter when they were written or by whom, as authoritative, impartial statements on the law. It must be emphasized that although law articles are usually carefully done and quite informative they are often written from a distinctive point of view; authors are often attempting to convince others of their viewpoint. Although such articles are stimulating they are not necessarily the viewpoint accepted by bench and bar.

It is common for particularly controversial legal issues to be represented by a number of competing perspectives. To obtain a balanced perspective, the student researcher should make every effort to read as many of these various viewpoints as possible. Only after a thorough reading should the student feel confident that he or she is in a position to evaluate the topic. As indicated earlier in this chapter, legal encyclopedias are an excellent source for impartial treatments of legal topics. Law periodicals, while full of valuable factual information, are best used to distinguish competing legal attitudes and values.

Because social scientists—and political scientists in particular—are interested in explaining the judicial process, law review articles are a source for understanding one of the outside influences brought to bear on judicial decisionmaking. Political scientist Chester A. Newland studied the references made to law review articles by justices of the U.S. Supreme Court. He found that during the period between 1926 and 1956 an average of about one fourth of the Court's opinions in a typical term cited between 40 and 70 law periodicals.[14] In other words, law article writing can serve as a subtle lobbying influence upon the courts. By reading these articles one can gain insight into how one form of judicial lobbying is conducted.

There are, of course, many articles which attempt objectivity and some are descriptive and explanatory in nature. But the discussion to this point should alert the student to the pitfalls of pulling a law journal off the shelf and treating its contents as gospel. It is obviously advisable to determine first which articles on a particular subject are available and then to choose and read from among them. The research tool making such a procedure possible is the *Index to Legal Periodicals*.

Index to Legal Periodicals

Published by the H. W. Wilson Company, the *Index to Legal Periodicals* started in 1926. It is the most complete index of legal periodicals published in the United States; it contains entries for articles appearing in legal journals in the United States, Canada, Great Britain, Ireland, Australia, and New Zealand. For articles before 1926 one must consult the *James-Chipman Index to Legal Periodicals*—a six-volume set for the period 1886–1937.[15] The *Index to Legal Periodicals* contains three main features: (1) subject and author index; (2) table of cases; and (3) book review index.

Subject and Author Index. Each cumulative volume and supplement contains a "List of Subject Headings." By first determining the subject heading that best describes one's research topic, the student can save considerable effort. For example, if interested in articles dealing with presidential impoundment of funds, one can find in the list of subject headings, "impoundment."

14. "Legal Periodicals and the U.S. Supreme Court," 3 *Midwest Journal of Political Science* 58–74 (February 1959).

15. J. Jacobstein and R. Mersky, *Fundamentals of Legal Research*, p. 314.

Turning alphabetically to "impoundment" in the subject and author index, numerous articles can be located.

Finding entries is slightly more complicated when interested in reading articles by a particular author. First, one locates in alphabetical order the last name of the author. Under the author's name is a listing of the subject headings under which his or her article(s) are classified. Turning to the appropriate subject heading(s) the author's name and article title are easily located. Depending upon the scope of the research project, it is advisable to consult a number of past and current volumes and to check the paperback supplementary indexes.

Following the article listings under each subject heading, case notes or discussions of recent cases relevant to the subject classification are listed under the title, "Cases." For example, in Volume 17 (September 1973–August 1976) following the list of articles under the subject heading "freedom of press," there is a list of four different case notes dealing with the topic. It first lists the case, followed by the name of the law journal, volume, page, and date of publication in which the case is discussed. These case notes, varying in length from merely a few to many pages, are often very helpful in interpreting what a particular case might mean.

Table of Cases Commented Upon. In addition to the listing of case discussions under the separate subject headings, there is the *Table of Cases Commented Upon.* Located at the back of each volume and supplement, this table lists each case alphabetically by plaintiff followed by the law journal entries. If a researcher is interested in finding what has been written about a particular case, this table is an excellent tool.

Book Review Index. This separate section of the *Index of Legal Periodicals* lists book reviews on legal subjects by name of author or title if the author's name is unkown.

Current Law Index

First appearing in 1980, *Current Law Index* (CLI) is a relatively new index sponsored by the American Association of Law Libraries and published by the Information Access Corporation. More than 660 periodicals are referenced and, in addition to the usual citations, it contains a few novel features. When appearing in an article, statutes are indexed by both their popular and official names. Books are graded in the book review section on a scale of A to F according to the response of the reviewer. As with other indexes, CLI is updated with periodic supplements.

Index to Foreign Legal Periodicals

For locating articles dealing with International law, Comparative law, and Municipal law of non-common law countries, the *Index to Foreign Legal Periodicals* is an available tool. Published by the Institute of Advanced Legal Studies of the University of London in Cooperation with the American Association of Law Libraries, this index contains article listings from 1960 to the present. It has an author index, subject index, geographical index, and book review index. The growing interest in comparative legal topics should make this index a valuable research tool for many years to come.

Index to Periodical Articles Related to Law

Commencing publication in 1958, this index was created to meet the growing recognition among lawyers of a need to apply the social and behavioral sciences to law. It includes English language articles which are of research value but do not appear in the *Index to Legal Periodicals* or the *Index to Foreign Legal Periodicals*. *Index to Periodical Articles Related to Law* is published quarterly and has a subject index, an index to articles, and an author index. It lists articles published which are of legal significance but appear in many journals not normally concerned with legal topics. For instance, this index includes articles from such unlikely places as the *Journal of Applied Psychology*, *Journal of Pastoral Care*, and the *Prison Journal*.

Before leaving the legal periodical topic, one additional note of caution should be sounded. There is a tendency for some students to pay special attention to a few law periodicals. Indeed it is true that some journals are particularly useful for certain studies. For example, the *Harvard Law Review* publishes an annual review of the Supreme Court's opinions; the *Emory Law Journal*, formerly known as the *Journal of Public Law*, is an excellent source for articles on public law topics; and the *Law and Society Review* is an extremely well done forum that brings together legal experts from a number of related disciplines. There are also journals devoted to specialized legal subjects such as the *American Journal of Legal History*, *Journal of Psychiatry and Law*, and *Journal of Law and Economics*. The danger with such a practice is that students sometimes ignore other articles of great value published in not so famous journals. The fact is that significant articles can be found in the most obscure journals and to ignore them is perilous. For a first rate research effort, always consult the various indexes.

LAW DICTIONARIES

A common complaint against the legal profession is that they have a language only lawyers can understand. There is some truth in this charge but law dictionaries are available to aid lay people and students. Most law dictionaries define a word or phrase in their legal sense and give citations to court decisions or other references. In this sense, law dictionaries are elementary research tools. Although they tend to be expensive, a law dictionary can be a useful acquisition.

Three widely known and employed law dictionaries are: (1) Ballentine, *Law Dictionary with Pronunciations,* 3rd Edition, Lawyers Cooperative Publishing Company, 1969; (2) Black, *Law Dictionary,* 5th Edition, West Publishing Company, 1979; (3) Bouvier, *Law Dictionary* (3rd revision), 8th Edition, West Publishing Company, 1914.

An excellent, less technical, and inexpensive dictionary is: Oran, *Law Dictionary for Non-Lawyers,* West Publishing Company, 1975.

KEEPING CURRENT

Anyone interested in legal topics should make an effort to be aware of recent developments. We like to think that most college educated persons have at least a passing awareness of the nature of the judicial process and are familiar with some of the Supreme Court's landmark decisions. Then, too, anyone actively pursuing a research project has an obligation to be aware of recent developments concerning his or her legal topic. However, keeping abreast of recent developments is not automatic and not as easy as might be supposed.

Newspapers and other media are the most obvious sources for information about current legal developments. Some newspapers and electronic media make a good attempt to provide readers, viewers, and listeners with accurate information. The *New York Times* and a growing number of leading newspapers often print the entire text or parts of the text of important Supreme Court opinions. However, most newspapers print summaries provided by news services. The stories received from the services are often edited by local newspapers reflecting space and cost considerations. The results of this editorial practice is often misleading information. Likewise the electronic media, while often employing highly qualified personnel, present misleading coverage due primarily to time allocated for such coverage. A common fault in media coverage is presenting dicta pronouncements as the rule of law.

The point of this discussion is to alert the student to be most careful in accepting news stories as accurate presentations of what really happens in courtrooms. It usually pays to read a court decision for one's self. The problem with such an approach is that it may take weeks or months to acquire a copy of a court decision. A publication which is a great aid in circumventing this problem is the *United States Law Week.*

U.S. Law Week

A publication of the Bureau of National Affairs, Inc., *U.S. Law Week* is a weekly looseleaf service designed to keep readers current on the weekly developments in the law. Its general features include: (1) a summary and analysis of new law and leading court cases of the preceding week; (2) new court decisions provided much earlier than any of the court reporters; (3) full text of federal statutes of general interest; and (4) a general news section giving readers advance notice of developments in pending or proposed legislation, administrative regulations, and litigation.

Law Week is divided into General and Supreme Court parts. The special binder devoted to the Supreme Court includes among its features: (1) full text and digests of Court decisions; (2) Supreme Court docket information; (3) orders granting or denying appellate review; (4) summaries of significant oral argument; and (5) summer issues analyze the work of the Court during the preceding term.

Because *Law Week* is divided into two separate sections, there are two indexes. Both indexes possess a topical descriptive index and a table of cases. They are easily employed.

There are other looseleaf services published by several companies. Most of these are very specialized, concerned with specific legal topics such as taxation, labor relations, or urban affairs.

LEGAL RESEARCH EXERCISES

The following exercises are designed to provide students with an initial "hands-on" experience with legal research materials. After the successful completion of these exercises students should feel confident that they are capable of initiating a research effort. Correct answers for the exercises are provided at the end of the chapter.

Exercise #1—Legal Encyclopedias

Part I. Employ *American Jurisprudence 2d.*
  1. What does the abbreviation Coven stand for?
  2. What is the subject *name* and *number* under which the suspension of the Writ of Habeas Corpus by the President is discussed?
  3. You are interested in learning about grounds for the issuance or dismissal of the writ of certiorari by the U.S. Supreme Court. What are the subject names and numbers under which such a discussion may be located?

Part II. Employ *Corpus Juris Secundum.*

You enter into an agreement with a landlord to lease an apartment. But at the last minute you find another place more to your liking. The landlord explains that if you do not rent his apartment as originally promised you will have breached the contract and are subject to a civil suit. Because you want to know something about landlord-tenant relations and "breach of contract" you decide to consult *Corpus Juris Secundum.*

4. In which General Index of *C.J.S.* is the subject of landlord and tenant indexed?
5. Under what subject-heading and section heading is the discussion of performance of breach of an agreement to lease found?

Exercise #2—Legal Codes

Part I. Employ *United States Code Service (USCS)*

You have been assigned the task of investigating federal legislation governing labor injunctions.

1. Under what Title of the Code is the subject found?
2. According to the "Research Guide" where in *Am. Jur. 2d* may a discussion of the answer for question 1 be found?
3. Under what numbered section of "Interpretive Notes and Decisions" may a specific discussion of race discrimination (as related to injunction) be found?

Part II. Employ *United States Code Annotated (USCA)*.

You are interested in learning about the statutory law concerning attorney fees in tort claims against the federal government.

4. Under what Title and Section may such a discussion be found?
5. What court decision addresses the problem of attorney fees for attorneys administering the estate of a deceased child?

Exercise #3—Digests

Part I. Employ the *American Digest System*.

1. Under what West Key Topic and Number may the case of *City of El Paso* v. *Simmons* (1965) be found?
2. You are interested in locating cases dealing with the tort of invasion of privacy relating to advertising. Under what West Key Topic and Number are the cases located?

Part II. Employ the *U.S. Supreme Court Digest* (West Publishing Co.)

3. In *City of El Paso* v. *Simmons* the U.S. Supreme Court discussed the topic of constitutional guarantees with respect to the obligation of contracts. What two U.S. Supreme Court cases between 1977 and 1979 were decided with respect to that issue?

Part III. Employ *U.S. Supreme Court Reports Digest: Lawyers' Edition*.

4. Under what subject heading(s) and section(s) is the case of *National League of Cities* v. *Usery* digested?
5. You are interested in the constitutional limitations of the commerce power. Which digest entry best digests this point?

Exercise #4—Citators

1. What are the three parallel citations for the U.S. Supreme Court case of *Katz* v. *U.S.* (1967)?

2. What does the abbreviation d mean?
3. Which is the first U.S. Supreme Court case in which *Katz* is cited in a dissenting opinion? (use the US citation only)
4. Which is the first case from any jurisdiction to distinguish *Katz*?
5. As of 1981, has the decision in *Katz* been overruled?

Exercise #5—Legal Periodicals

Part I. Employ the *Index to Legal Periodicals.*
1. Beginning in 1970 and ending in 1976, list the articles written by Robert A. Mello.
2. What are the various subheadings for the subject "Legal Profession" in the *Index to Legal Periodicals?*
3. As of 1979, approximately how many different comments have been written on the case of *National League of Cities* v. *Usery?*
4. For the years 1963 to 1970, list the reviews written of Edmond Cahn's book, *Great Rights* (1963).

Part II. Employ the *Index to Periodical Articles Related to Law.*
5. Between 1969 and 1978, what is the subject heading under which an article written by E. M. Goldberg is indexed?

ANSWERS FOR LEGAL EXERCISES

Exercise #1—Legal Encyclopedias

1. Covenants, Conditions, and Restrictions.
2. Hab Corp §§ 6, 7.
3. Fed Prac §§ 281–289, § 325; Courts § 9.
4. General Index F–L.
5. Landlord and Tenant § 196 (1). See also, §§ 196 (1)–196 (4); § 249, § 104.

Exercise #2—Legal Codes

1. 29 – Labor
2. 42 Am. Jur. 2d, Injunctions § 74; 48 Am. Jur. 2d, Labor and Labor Relations §§ 1440–1524.
3. 29 USCS 104, section 35 (page 84).
4. Title 28, § 2678.
5. *Hodges v. U.S.* D.C. Iowa 1948, 98 F. Supp. 281.

Exercise #3—Digests

1. Const. Law 12, 81, 113, 117, 123, 154 (1), 169; Courts 383 (1); Public Lands 176 (2); States 4.4.
2. Torts 8

3. *United States Trust Company of New York v. New Jersey* 431 U.S. 1 (1977); *Allied Structural Steel Company v. Spannaus* 428 U.S. 234 (1978).
4. Com §§ 62, 63, 89, 96, 108; Const. L. §§ 48, 513, 861.5; Jury § 2; States §§ 5, 16, 34, 37.
5. Com § 63.

Exercise #4—Citators

1. 389 U.S. 347; 88 S. Ct. 507, 19 L.Ed 2d 576.
2. (distinguished)—case is different either in terms of fact or law.
3. 394 US 187.
4. 390 F 2d 371.
5. No.

Exercise #5—Legal Periodicals

1. "Public Utility Rate Increases: A Practice Manual for Administrative Litigation." *Clearinghouse Review* 8: 411–23 0 '74.
2. Bar Association, Integrated Bar; Legal Ethics, Paraprofessional Public Relations; Unauthorized Practice of Law.
3. Over 40.
4. A. M. Bendich, Calif. L. Rev. 51: 651 Ag. '63.
5. Privacy.

2

Survey of Book Literature

Books that elaborate upon judicial decisions in a variety of ways are important aids in legal research. This is particularly true for students of the social sciences. Excessive reliance upon court reports, encyclopedias, digests, codes, and citators tends to narrow legal research to the ascertainment of legal rules. Those interested in obtaining a wide appreciation and knowledge of the role of law in human society must step back from the legal minutiae to observe the totality of law in society. While it is necessary to become aware of legal rules, it is also important to understand the origins, decisional politics, and impacts of these rules. Books permitting students to view the forest through the trees are a necessary research tool without which a myopic vision of the judicial system surely results.

Classifying available books on constitutional law topics is a risky business. Most authors are eclectic in their approaches and as a consequence there is considerable overlap and mixing of systems and methods. In the most general and introductory of ways, the classification presented here is intended only to steer students to available literature useful when researching a topic for a typical undergraduate constitutional law course. Also, the book annotations to follow are by no means a complete list of available titles in constitutional law, judicial process, or behavior. Works of some favorite authors will no doubt be omitted. Regretably, however, it is not possible to annotate all the fine books in a volume of this size. The annotations should therefore be viewed as a sample of available titles, to be supplemented by the selected bibliography in Chapter 6 of this book and the reader's own search of the literature.

EXPOSITORY WORKS

Authors of expository books attempt to describe, explain, and interpret the entire field or subfield of constitutional law. These books are intended to appeal to a wide scholarly or student audience and are often written in the hope that they will be adopted for course use.

Most often casebooks are employed by instructors as the sole text. These casebooks typically include brief introductions to each constitutional law topic, followed by a number of edited judicial opinions. Although casebooks possess pedagogical merit, they often fail to adequately tie the disparate materials together. The following annotated list of books is valuable because it integrates subject material in a clear fashion. One note of caution must be sounded, however. These expository works are often outdated the day they are published. Because the work of courts never ends, new judicial opinions are sometimes delivered that render old precedents obsolete. This is a fundamental reason why books cannot be the sole source for legal research. However, if a particular work has been well received, new editions or supplements updating the previous work are often published.

The entries are in chronological order.

The American Constitutional System, 5th ed. C. Herman Pritchett. New York: McGraw-Hill Book Company, 1981.
    A succinct account of the entire constitutional system. Provides an excellent overview of the subject matter.

Liberty in the Balance: Current Issues in Civil Liberties, 5th ed. H. Frank Way. New York: McGraw-Hill Book Company, 1981.
    An absorbing treatment of racial discrimination, womens rights, gay rights, press and censorship, speech, religion, and criminal justice. Integrates case law with relevant social, political, and economic data and analysis.

The Supreme Court and Individual Rights. Elder Witt, ed. Washington, D.C.: Congressional Quarterly, Inc., 1980.
    A fine treatment of the Court's role in protecting individual liberties and rights. Topics include: speech; religion; political participation; due process; racial alienage; sexual; and income discrimination. Excellent narrative with citation to relevant cases.

Congressional Quarterly's Guide to the U.S. Supreme Court. Congressional Quarterly. Washington, D.C.: Congressional Quarterly, Inc., 1979.
    An outstanding reference work of more than 1,000 pages. It contains information on all aspects of the Supreme Court. Topics include: the Court history; the Court and federalism; the Court and presidential power; the Court and judicial power; the Court and the states; the Court, civil liberties, and rights; the political pressures on the Court; the internal operations of the Court; and the major decisions of the Court.

Constitutional Law: A Textbook, 2d ed. Bernard Schwartz. New York: Macmillan Publishing Co., Inc., 1979.

A good interpretive narration on all constitutional law topics typically covered in law school courses. Discussion includes decisions through the October 1977 Supreme Court term.

Corwin and Peltason's Understanding the Constitution. 8th ed. J. W. Peltason. New York: Holt, Rinehart and Winston, 1979.

A nontechnical discussion of the main features of the Constitution and its historical and practical significance as applied today.

American Constitutional Law. Laurence H. Tribe. Mineola, New York: The Foundation Press, Inc., 1978. Also available in two paperback editions: *The Constitutional Structure of American Government: Separation and Division of Powers;* and *The Constitutional Protection of Individual Rights: Limits of Government's Authority.*

A massive examination of almost every aspect of constitutional interpretation. Author builds seven analytical models of constitutional law providing not only a summary of Supreme Court decisions but also a system for thinking about them. Author makes no attempt to hide his value judgments and in particular his distaste for the Burger Court, but also attempts to present opposing views.

The Constitution and What It Means Today. Edward S. Corwin, Revised by Harold W. Chase and Craig R. Ducat. 14th ed. Princeton, N.J.: Princeton University Press, 1978.

An authoritative summary of the interpretation of the Constitution, article by article and amendment by amendment. Now in its fourteenth edition it is widely used as a quick reference by those interested in the Court's interpretation of the Constitution.

Handbook on Constitutional Law. John E. Nowak, Ronald D. Rotunda, and J. Nelson Young. St. Paul, Minn.: West Publishing Co., 1978.

Making no attempt to cover the entire field of constitutional law, this is a fine treatment of Supreme Court adjudication in areas of contemporary interest to constitutional law students. Supplemented annually.

Modes of Constitutional Interpretation. Craig R. Ducat. St. Paul, Minn.: West Publishing Co., 1978.

An analysis of the principal frameworks employed by justices of the Supreme Court in justifying their opinions. Author deals with judicial review, absolutism, balancing of interests, and the preferred freedoms approach. Issues discussed are of great contemporary interest.

The American Constitution. 3rd ed. C. Herman Pritchett. New York: McGraw Hill Book Company, 1977.

An analytical examination of the Supreme Court's interpretation of the Constitution. It covers most constitutional provisions of interest and provides an understanding of the politics surrounding court decisions.

Freedom and the Court: Civil Rights and Liberties in the United States. 3rd ed. Henry J. Abraham. New York: Oxford University Press, 1977.

An analysis of the conflict between individual rights and the community welfare. Excellent historical discussion of the process of incorporation of the Bill of Rights by way of the Fourteenth Amendment. A skillful discussion of religion, speech, due process, and political and racial equality. Excellent overview of the political development of civil liberties and rights in the United States.

Presidential Power in a Nutshell. Arthur S. Miller. St. Paul, Minn.: West Publishing Co., 1977.

A brief exposition on the law and politics of the presidency. Covers all important legal topics and emphasizes that presidential power cannot be understood through a purely legal approach.

The Defendant's Rights Today. David Fellman. Madison, Wisconsin: The University of Wisconsin Press, 1976.

A first-rate discussion of the Supreme Court's handling of criminal justice cases. Excellent historical explanations of why criminal justice is tilted in favor of defendants. Topics covered are: arrests, preliminary hearing; bail; habeas corpus, trial by jury; right to counsel; searches and seizures, self-incrimination; double jeopardy; and cruel and unusual punishment.

The Supreme Court and the Commander in Chief (expanded edition). Clinton Rossiter with additional text by Richard P. Longaker. Ithaca, New York: Cornell University Press, 1976.

A classic study of how the Supreme Court has interpreted presidential war powers.

The Constitution of the United States of America: Analysis and Interpretation. Prepared by the Congressional Research Service, Library of Congress. Washington, D.C.: U.S. Government Printing Office, 1973. Senate Document No. 92–82.

A very lengthy, authoritative, and narrative exposition of the Constitution, clause by clause. The first edition was published in 1913. Contains annual pocket supplements.

HISTORICAL ACCOUNTS OF THE SUPREME COURT

Every student of constitutional law soon learns that the meaning of the Constitution is not fixed in time. Rather, it has changed over time, with each court making its own contribution. Reflecting the values and attitudes of the members of the Supreme Court, courts from the time of John Jay and John Marshall to Earl Warren and Warren Burger have left their own impressions upon the constitutional edifice. Possessing leeway but not license, courts have looked to the past, present, and future for guidance in their decisionmaking; differing perceptions have sometimes resulted in conflicting conclusions.

Any book dealing with constitutional law must necessarily consider historical evolution. But court histories are usually explicit attempts to understand the development of the law through an analysis of how various courts have contributed in their own manner to the meaning of the Constitution. Court histories may attempt to understand the Constitution in several ways. Some works discuss the entire history of the Supreme Court from the formation of the Union to the present. Others are in-depth studies of particular courts and some are comparisons of various courts. Many studies concentrate on how the various courts have dealt with particular constitutional provisions or doctrines. Whatever the variation, court histories are valuable because they provide an overall perspective other books often fail to convey.

The First Freedom: The Tumultuous History of Free Speech in America. Nat Hentoff. New York: Delacorte Press, 1980.

A well written history and detailed discussion of leading Supreme Court cases involving speech, press, and religion.

World War I and the Origin of Civil Liberties in the United States. Paul L. Murphy. New York: W. W. Norton, 1980.

A very interesting argument that the development of civil liberties as a body of law did not occur before the coming of World War I.

Judges and Justices: The Federal Appellate Judiciary. John R. Schmidhauser. Boston: Little, Brown and Co., 1979.

Most properly classified as an important book in judicial process, this effort contains two chapters of particular historical interest—a study of the social and political backgrounds of the justices of the Supreme Court and federal appellate court judges, 1789–1976; and a discussion of the evolution of the Supreme Court's internal procedures.

Constitutional Counterrevolution? The Warren and the Burger Courts Judicial Political Making in Modern America. Richard Y. Funston. New York: Halsted Press, 1977.

A critical analysis of the judicial decisions of the Warren and Burger Courts. Excellent discussion of the uses of judicial self-restraint.

The American Constitution: Its Origins and Development. 5th ed. Alfred Kelly and Winfred A. Harbinson. New York: Norton, 1976.

Now in its fifth edition, this fine volume is a basic text on the history of the U.S. Constitution. Covers materials from colonial days to the present.

A Selected Bibliography of American Constitutional History. Stephen M. Millett. Santa Barbara, Calif.: Clio Books, 1975.

An excellent bibliography covering every facet of constitutional history. Also contains a fine section on judicial biographies.

The Role of the Supreme Court in American Government and Politics 1789–1835. Charles Grove Haines. New York: De Capo Press, 1957; *The Role of the Supreme Court in American Government and Politics 1835–1864.* Charles Grove Haines and Foster H. Sherwood. Berkeley and Los Angeles: University of California Press, 1973.

These two volumes represent a monument to careful scholarship. Authors undertake to demonstrate that the Supreme Court is fundamentally a political institution.

The Supreme Court in Crisis: A History of Conflict. Robert J. Steamer. Amherst, Mass.: University of Massachusetts Press, 1971.

An interesting history of the Supreme Court as the nonelected branch pitted against the popularly elected branches of government.

1787: The Grand Convention. Clinton Rossiter. New York: Macmillan, 1966.

A splendid treatment of the Philadelphia Convention with an account of ratification politics.

The Records of the Federal Convention of 1787, 4 Vols. Max Farrand, ed. New Haven, Conn.: Yale University Press, 1911/1937/1966.

Contains the daily records of the Constitutional Convention. Providing researchers with the ability to trace the origin and development of particular clauses, the index found in volume 4 includes references for every clause finally adopted.

The American Supreme Court. Robert G. McCloskey. Chicago: University of Chicago Press, 1960.

A historical treatment of the Supreme Court emphasizing judicial review.

Supreme Court Review. Philip B. Kurland. 3rd ed. Chicago: University of Chicago Press, 1960.

This is an annual publication reviewing the major work of the Supreme Court for each term of the court since 1960. Essays are written on pertinent topics by law professors and political scientists. May also be classified as a law review.

Nine Men: A Political History of the Supreme Court from 1790–1955. Fred Rodell. New York: Random House, 1955.

A history of the Supreme Court from the era of John Jay to Earl Warren. Powerful in its attempt to view the Court as a political institution and in its argument that the Court has most often reflected conservative political values.

American Constitutional Development. Carl B. Swisher. Boston: Houghton Mifflin, 1954.

An excellent historical treatment of constitutional issues, which is especially useful for understanding constitutional problems in the first part of this century.

The Roosevelt Court. C. Herman Pritchett. New York: Macmillan, 1948.

Recognized as the one book which more than any other revolutionized the study of the judicial process. Author focuses on the Supreme Court from 1937–1947. Analyzing the nonunanimous votes of the justices, the author studies the politics, attitudes, and values of the Roosevelt Court.

The Federalist: A Commentary on the Constitution of the United States. [Alexander Hamilton, James Madison, and John Jay]. Edward Meade Earle, ed. New York: The Modern Library, 1941.

Eighty-five essays that advocated the adoption of the Constitution. The essays were written under "Publius" by Alexander Hamilton, James Madison, and John Jay and appeared in New York newspapers. These essays became widely known and had an impact on the ratification debates around the United States. The Papers are sometimes cited by courts and others as evidence of the Founding Fathers' intent. Available in a number of editions.

The Supreme Court in United States History, 2 vols. Charles Warren. Boston: Little, Brown and Company, 1937.

Careful and perceptive work in constitutional history with special attention to the interplay of politics and history with the law.

JUDICIAL BIOGRAPHIES

Judicial biographies are typically absorbing accounts of the life and times of individual justices. Although modern social science methods have been employed in an attempt to comprehend judicial attitudes and values, judicial biographies are often a valuable contribution in supplementing and sometimes in correcting our notions of the motivations underlying judicial opinions. Besides teaching us about decisionmaking, judicial biographies are instructive as to career patterns and the character of those acceding to the Supreme Court.

Lawyers and judges in particular have a tendency to retain their personal correspondence and records. Historians and political scientists who gain access to these papers are able to fill in many details surrounding the judicial environment—information which would otherwise remain closeted behind the purple curtain. Biographers make use of published material, private papers, and personal interviews where possible. Most of the better biographies have been written about well known twentieth century judges and a handful of nineteenth century jurists. Some are autobiographical. A shortcoming to be on the alert for is the tendency by some authors to idealize or at least overemphasize the accomplishments and character of the studied justice.

The Enigma of Felix Frankfurter. H. N. Hirsch. New York: Basic Books, 1981.

An example of psychobiography. Focuses upon the personality of this controversial justice; the author analyzes Frankfurter as a liberal New Dealer and how he became an isolated figure on the High Court.

The Court Years, 1939-1975: The Autobiography of William O. Douglas. William O. Douglas. New York: Random House, 1980.

Compared to *Go East, Young Man* (See below), this autobiographical account is a disappointment. Sprinkled with short expositions on prominent public figures Douglas knew during a 36-year Court tenure, the book does provide some insight into his judicial philosophy.

Independent Journey: The Life of William O. Douglas. James F. Simon. New York: Harper and Row, 1980.

An admiring, highly readable, and excellent portrait. Author presents sufficient information for readers to draw a negative conclusion about Douglas.

Mr. Justice Black: Absolutist on the Court. James L. Magee. Charlottesville, Virginia: University of Virginia Press, 1980.

An intriguing study tracing Black's First Amendment views from the initial preferred position doctrine, to his absolutist period and finally to his less libertarian position in his later years.

Hugo Black and the Judicial Revolution. Gerald Dunne. New York: Simon and Schuster, 1977.

Excellent treatment of Black's days in Alabama, the U.S. Senate, and his long years on the Supreme Court.

The Memoirs of Earl Warren. Earl Warren. Garden City, N.Y.: Doubleday and Co., 1977.

An autobiographical view of how Warren saw himself and the people and events that surrounded his fifty years of public service. Excellent account of Warren's troubles with such foes as the American Bar Association and the John Birch Society. Warren died before this book was completed.

Go East, Young: The Early Years. William O. Douglas. New York: Random House, 1974.

This is an interesting and revealing autobiography depicting the early struggles and associates of the opinionated Douglas. His candid appraisal of Felix Frankfurter and other New Dealers is most instructive.

Private Pressure on Public Law: The Legal Career of Justice Thurgood Marshall. Randall W. Bland. Port Washington, N.Y.: Kennikat Press, 1973.

This biography examines the life of the first black to sit on the Supreme Court bench; a fascinating account of Marshall's association with the NAACP and his days as U.S. Solicitor General. There is a discussion of Marshall's judicial opinions. However, more years will have to pass before a definitive judgment can be made about Marshall's effectiveness on the Court.

The Justices of the United States Supreme Court 1789–1969: Their Lives and Major Opinions, 4 vols. Leon Friedman and Fred L. Israel, eds. New York and London: Chelsea House Publishers, 1969.

This is a massive effort to record the lives and important opinions of every member of the Supreme Court from 1798 to 1969. It is the most complete work of its kind and provides a valuable bibliography of available articles and books on each justice.

Mr. Justice. Allison Dunham and Philip B. Kurland, eds. Chicago: Phoenix Books, The University of Chicago Press, 1964.

A valuable collection of short biographies about 12 Supreme Court justices written by outstanding public law scholars. Contains biographies of Marshall, Taney, Bradley, Harlan, Holmes, Hughes, Brandeis, Sutherland, Stone, Cardozo, Murphy, and Rutledge.

William Howard Taft: Chief Justice. Alpheus Thomas Mason. London: Oldbourne Book Co. Ltd., 1964.

Interesting account of the life of the only man to be both President of the United States and Chief Justice of the Supreme Court. A conservative and opponent of government regulation, Taft was primarily responsible for remodeling the federal judicial system.

Morrison R. Waite: The Triumph of Character. C. Peter Magrath. New York: Macmillan, 1963.

A warm but objective treatment of Chief Justice Waite from his early years in Connecticut and later in Ohio to his management of the Supreme Court during an important period of U.S. history, 1874–1887.

Harlan Fiske Stone: Pillar of the Law. Alpheus Thomas Mason. New York: Viking Press, 1956.

Going beyond historical description, the author utilizes Stone's personal papers and interviews with Stone's associates. Also serves as an excellent history of the Supreme Court for the period 1925–1946. This penetrating work is generally viewed as the best, or at least one of the finest, judicial biographies ever written.

The Life of John Marshall, 4 vols. Albert J. Beveridge. New York: Houghton Mifflin Company, 1916–1919.

A detailed account of Marshall's life employing personal letters, diaries and journals, newspapers of the time, and other sources. Author emphasizes Marshall's strong points.

CASE STUDIES

Rather than simply reporting or interpreting a Supreme Court decision, the authors of case studies endeavor to view the total environment. This is accomplished typically by tracing the beginnings of a case—may it originate in a police station, a corporate board room, or on the picket line—and then follow the case through the maze of the various political and judicial channels, ending with a discussion of the impact of the case. Such studies provide readers with the full scope and intimate knowledge useful in understanding the dynamics of constitutional politics.

Case studies suffer from a major deficiency. Such studies may fully explain a case in all its relevant parts, making it difficult at best to generalize from the one case to the broader political system. Yet, with this shortcoming in mind, case studies can provide the reader with a feel for constitutional politics unrivaled by any other type of book. Although the potential list of case studies is long, here are annotations of some of the many well done works.

Bakke, DeFunis, and Minority Admissions: The Quest for Equal Opportunity. Allan P. Sindler. New York: Longman, Inc., 1978.

An in-depth treatment of two highly controversial affirmative action cases dealing with so-called reverse discrimination. These law and medical school admission cases illustrate the interaction of government and university bureaucracies and the courts.

The Supreme Court and Civil Liberties Policy. Richard C. Cortner, Palo Alto, California: Mayfield Publishing Co., 1975.

Intended as a supplementary text, the author provides six in-depth studies of recent Supreme Court cases involving the nationalization of the Bill of Rights. Cases discussed are: *Duncan* v. *Louisiana; Doe* v. *Bolton; Chimel* v. *California; Cohen* v. *California; Wisconsin* v. *Yoder;* and *Frontiero* v. *Richardson.*

The Steamboat Monopoly: Gibbons v. Ogden, 1824. Maurice G. Baxter. New York: Alfred A. Knopf, 1972.

Places the first case to interpret the commerce clause in its political and economic context. It investigates the impact of *Gibbons* upon nineteenth century America and discusses the long-range importance of the case.

Scottsboro: A Tragedy of the American South. Dan T. Carter. New York: Oxford University Press, 1971.

An award winning account of the infamous Scottsboro cases. It is a vivid account of radicalism, racism, and southern justice during the 1930s.

The Jones and Laughlin Case. Richard C. Cortner. New York: Alfred A. Knopf, 1970.

For those interested in the history of the commerce clause, this case study is must reading.

Yazoo: Law and Politics in the New Republic. C. Peter Magrath. New York: Norton, 1967.

An interesting study of the famous case of *Fletcher* v. *Peck.* For those who think corruption is new to the United States, this study will be enlightening. Case study followed by an excellent brief history of the contract clause.

It Is So Ordered: The Supreme Court Rules on School Segregation. Daniel M. Berman. New York: Norton, 1966.

This is an excellent treatment of the famous cases of *Brown* v. *Board of Education.* A good introduction for beginning students to the workings of the judicial system.

Wiretapping on Trial: A Case Study in the Judicial Process. Walter F. Murphy. New York: Random House, 1965.

This is a study of the case of *Olmstead* v. *United States.* Deals with this important case from the first trial through Supreme Court adjudication and has a good, but not outdated, discussion of the law involving wiretapping.

Gideon's Trumpet. Anthony Lewis. New York: Vintage Books, 1964.

A very readable account of the landmark right to counsel case, *Gideon* v. *Wainwright.*

The Third Branch of Government: 8 Cases in Constitutional Politics. C. Herman Pritchett and Alan F. Westin, eds. New York: Harcourt, Brace and World, Inc., 1963.

This is an excellent collection of case studies dealing with eight Supreme Court decisions occurring since 1937. Studies written by eight different authors include: the flag-salute case; the portal-to-portal case, the electric chair case; the released time case; the NAACP in Alabama; subversion and the cold war; the offshore oil cases; and the Sunday closing cases.

The Anatomy of a Constitutional Law Case. Alan F. Westin. New York: Macmillan, 1958.

For over two decades one of the most widely read case studies. A portrait of the famous steel seizure case known as *Youngstown Sheet and Tube* v. *Sawyer,* it vividly records how this case rose from a bargaining dispute to the intervention of various governmental agencies and the role of the judiciary.

IMPACT ANALYSIS

Closely related to, and to some extent overlapping, case studies are those works most specifically interested in analyzing the impact of court decisions.

It is one thing to understand what a court has said and why it has said it, but it is quite another matter to ascertain what happens after a decision is handed down. The fact is that compliance with a judicial opinion is not automatic and simply because the Supreme Court hands down a judgment does not necessarily mean that the political controversy is over. A cursory examination of the history of the Supreme Court's efforts to end segregation in the public schools or the public reaction to the Court's abortion decision should alert even the most casual observer to the difficulties involved in compliance. Moreover, the myth that the Supreme Court is the final place to appeal policy decisions should be arrested by the observation that Court decisions can be overturned through constitutional amendment, passage of new statutory language, or the removal of appellate jurisdiction.

Published in law or social science journals, most impact studies appear in article form. However, because political scientists have in recent years acquired a greater interest in policy studies, there is a growing list of available books employing impact analysis. Although some authors have attempted to construct adequate theoretical frameworks, it does not appear that impact analysis has progressed to the point where suitable paradigms may be employed. Yet the available studies point the way to a better understanding of constitutional politics. Here is an annotated list of some of the better impact studies on hand in book form.

The Impact of Reapportionment. Timothy G. O'Rourke. New Brunswick, N.J.: Transaction Books, 1979.

The latest in a long line of studies to consider the impact of *Baker* v. *Carr* and other reapportionment decisions on state politics. Six states are used as the basis for analysis.

Judicial Impact and State Supreme Courts. George Alan Tarr. Lexington, Mass.: Lexington Books, 1977.

An empirical investigation of state compliance with 97 U.S. Supreme Court Establishment Clause cases decided between 1947 and 1973. Author presents interesting alternative explanations for compliance and noncompliance.

The Impact of Supreme Court Decisions. 2d ed. Theodore L. Becker and Malcolm M. Feeley, eds. New York: Oxford University Press, 1973.

A fine collection of articles originally appearing in law and social science journals dealing with a variety of impact topics. A number of articles appear under the following general headings, preceded by the editors' explanatory introductions: the Court's effect on the President and Congress; the Supreme Court's impact on lower federal courts; the Court's impact on state and local government and politics; and the Court's impact on public opinion. A final section deals with the theory and methods of impact analysis.

Public Evaluation of Constitutional Courts: Alternative Explanations. Walter F. Murphy, Joseph Tanenhaus, and Daniel L. Kastner. Sage Professional Paper in Comparative Politics Series, Number 01-045. Beverly Hills, Calif.: Sage Publications, 1973.

This is a slim but highly technical and informative volume concerning the ability of constitutional courts to have an impact upon public opinion. The findings, based upon survey data from the mid-1960s, are generally negative. Serious students of public opinion and the courts will find this work important.

Law and Social Change: Civil Rights Laws and Their Consequences. Harrell R. Rodgers, Jr. and Charles S. Bullock, III. New York: McGraw-Hill Book Company, 1972.

A study of the impact of legislative and judicial decisions upon the rights of blacks. Deals with voting, public accommodations, school desegregation, employment, and housing.

The Supreme Court and Congress: Conflict and Interaction, 1945-1968. John R. Schmidhauser and Larry L. Berg. New York: The Free Press, 1972.

Employing both historical and modern behavioral methods, the authors investigate the myth that the Supreme Court is protected from congressional attack by an aura of reverence. Excellent discussion of the role of lawyer-congressmen and the American Bar Association in Court/Congress inter-institutional conflicts.

The Court and Local Law Enforcement: The Impact of Miranda. Neil A. Milner. Beverly Hills, California: Sage Publications, 1971.

This fine book assesses the impact of the Supreme Court's decision in *Miranda* v. *Arizona* upon four Wisconsin police departments.

The Impact of the United States Supreme Court: Some Perspectives. Stephen L. Wasby. Homewood, Ill.: The Dorsey Press, 1970.

An excellent effort to bring together and integrate the various works on impact. Author discusses problems of conceptualization and offers a series of hypotheses for future research.

Community Conflict, Public Opinion and the Law: The Amish Dispute in Iowa. Harrell R. Rodgers, Jr. Columbus, Ohio: Charles E. Merrill Publishing Company, 1969.

This is a case study of a legal dispute that did not reach the U. S. Supreme Court. The author employing modern political science techniques concerns himself with the circumstances under which responsible officials refuse to enforce the law and what effect such refusal has upon public support for law and the political system generally.

The Dynamics of Compliance: Supreme Court Decision-Making From A New Perspective. Richard M. Johnson. Evanston, Ill.: Northwestern University Press, 1967.

Author develops an interesting analytical framework within which to study compliance. The study focuses upon the politics of compliance with the Supreme Court's school prayer decisions in two Illinois rural school districts.

Prayer in the Public Schools: Law and Attitude Change. William K. Muir, Jr. Chicago: University of Chicago Press, 1967.

A before-and-after study of educator reactions to the Supreme Court school prayer decisions. The application of psychological cognitive dissonance theory to the issue of whether law can change deeply rooted attitudes.

Desegregation and the Law: The Meaning and Effect of the School Segregation Cases. Albert P. Blaustein and Clarence Clyde Ferguson, Jr. New York: Vintage Books, 1962.

An early example of an impact study. Combines the case study feature of tracing the development of the case(s) through the Supreme Court, with an excellent description of the problems of compliance, avoidance and delay. A study of the impact of legislation and judicial decisions upon the rights of blacks. Deals with voting, public accommodations, school desegregation, employment, and housing.

JUDICIAL PROCESS AND BEHAVIOR

Thus far the annotated list of books has included works of particular substantive value for studying constitutional law. However, the study of judicial process and behavior is an important area in the field of public law and may be studied in conjunction with or as part of a course in constitutional law. As a matter of fact, it has been seriously argued that not constitutional law per se, but judicial process and behavior is the proper focus of study. Whatever one's preference, there can be little doubt that studies concentrating upon how and why judges make decisions, the demands and supports upon the judicial system, and the politics and policies surrounding the judiciary are necessary for an understanding of how government works.

Judicial process and behavior books range from simple institutional descriptions of how the judicial process works to, for example, sophisticated treatments invoking approaches such as small group, psychometric, interest group, or role analysis. The annotations that follow feature a limited number of these works including collections of articles appearing in book form.

Courts, Law, and Judicial Processes. S. Sidney Ulmer, ed. New York: The Free Press, 1981.

A collection of 80 articles focusing on decisionmaking discretion, structure, and purposes of judicial institutions, and current problems in the judicial system. Most of the edited articles are reprinted from previously published works.

The Constitutions of the Communist World. William B. Simons, ed. Alphen ann den Rijn, Germantown, Md.: Sijthoff & Noordhoff, 1980.

A translation of the constitutions of 15 Communist nation-states. Introductory essays written by subject specialists precede each document.

The Judicial Process: An Introductory Analysis of the Courts of the United States, England, and France. 4th ed. Henry J. Abraham. New York: Oxford University Press, 1980.

An excellent treatment of the judicial systems of the U.S., England, and France. Also includes some discussion of the judicial system in the U.S.S.R. Fine discussion of judicial self-restraint as practiced in the United States. Contains a thorough bibliography.

The Brethren: Inside the Supreme Court. Bob Woodward and Scott Armstrong. New York: Simon & Schuster, 1979.

A highly controversial journalistic account about the internal politics of the Burger Court. The authors claim to rely on confidential interviews of former Supreme Court clerks.

Courts, Judges, and Politics: An Introduction to the Judicial Process. 3rd ed. Walter F. Murphy and C. Herman Pritchett, eds. New York: Random House, 1979.

A good collection of edited cases and articles covering most aspects of the judicial process in the U.S.

American Court Systems: Readings in Judicial Process and Behavior. Sheldon Goldman and Austin Sarat, eds. San Francisco: W.H. Freeman and Company, 1978.

A selection of 54 articles placed in a dispute-processing framework. Contains many of the finest articles ever written in the field of judicial process and behavior.

An Introduction to the Courts and Judicial Process. Merlin Lewis, Warren Bundy, and James L. Hague. Englewood Cliffs, New Jersey: Prentice-Hall, Inc., 1978.

A good introduction to the courts and the criminal justice system.

The Supreme Court in the Federal Judicial System. Stephen L. Wasby. New York: Holt, Rinehart and Winston, 1978.

A text designed to inform about the operations and roles of the U.S. Supreme Court. A good discussion of the effects of Supreme Court decisions on American life.

Comparative Constitutional Law: Cases and Commentaries. Walter F. Murphy and Joseph Tanenhaus. New York: St. Martin's Press, 1977.

The first text of its kind. Discusses the politics and courts of six nation-states and then presents judicial opinions of these courts classified under the following headings: horizontal and vertical distribution of power; foreign affairs; governmental regulation of economic affairs; equality under law; human dignity and public health, morals and safety; religious freedom; freedom of expression; voting and political participation; threats to a democratic order; and constitutions in times of emergency. The six countries studied are U.S., Germany, Japan, Canada, Australia, and Ireland.

Judicial Administration: Text and Readings. Russell R. Wheeler and Howard R. Whitcomb. Englewood Cliffs, New Jersey: Prentice-Hall, 1977.

A much needed text that brings together the important and growing literature in this developing field of study and employment.

Lawyers, Public Policy and Interest Group Politics. Albert P. Melone. Washington, D.C.: University Press of America, 1977.

A study of the sociology and politics of the American Bar Association and its relationship with government and other vital segments of society.

Supreme Court Decision-Making. David W. Rohde and Harold J. Spaeth. San Francisco: W.H. Freeman and Company, 1976.

A valuable example of the judicial behavior approach to the study of Supreme Court decisionmaking.

Unequal Justice: Lawyers and Social Change in Modern America. Jerold S. Auerbach. New York: Oxford University Press, 1976.

A lively and penetrating account of how the elite segment of the bar dominates the legal profession and has fought against social change.

Human Jurisprudence: Public Law as Political Science. Glendon Schubert. Honolulu: The University Press of Hawaii, 1975.

As a leading advocate of the judicial behavior approach, the author in one volume provides an overall view of public law and his pioneering efforts to develop public law as a first-rate social science. Author is responsible for more than 100 publications and this book permits readers in one source to understand the thinking of this outstanding scholar.

American Judicial Process: Models and Approaches. Charles H. Sheldon. New York: Dodd, Mead and Company, 1974.

A fine discussion of the analytical models and conceptual approaches developed for studying the judiciary.

The Judicial Mind Revisited: Psychometric Analysis of Supreme Court Ideology. Glendon Schubert. New York: Oxford University Press, 1974.

Focusing primarily upon methodology, the author develops a theory of political ideology from a synthesis of the works of leading psychologists. Studies ideological patterns of justices from the Vinson through the Warren eras.

State Court Systems. Henry Robert Glick and Kenneth N. Vines. Englewood Cliffs, New Jersey: Prentice-Hall, Inc., 1973.

A slim but important contribution that brings the study of state judicial systems into focus.

Lawyers Before the Warren Court: Civil Liberties and Civil Rights, 1957–66. Jonathan D. Casper. Urbana, Ill.: University of Illinois Press, 1972.

This work explores how private practice attorneys become involved in litigation before the Supreme Court and what goals and interests they pursue.

The Study of Public Law. Walter F. Murphy and Joseph Tanenhaus. New York: Random House, 1972.

An excellent review of the developments and approaches in the discipline of public law. Authors employ the growing number of cross-cultural studies.

Comparative Judicial Politics: The Political Functionings of Courts. Theodore L. Becker. Chicago: Rand McNally and Co., 1970.

Author attempts a reconceptualization of public law applying concepts of structure and function. Argues for a better understanding of judicial role as opposed to judicial behavior.

The Politics of Federal Courts: Lower Courts in the United States. Richard J. Richardson and Kenneth N. Vines. Boston: Little, Brown and Company, 1970.

Explores the role of lower federal courts in the judicial system. Presents evidence exploding the myth of a judicial hierarchy.

Comparative Judicial Behavior: Cross-Cultural Studies of Political Decision-Making in the East and West. Glendon Schubert and David J. Danelski, eds. New York: Oxford University Press, 1969.

An outstanding collection of articles dealing with judicial behavior studies of Korea, Japan, Philippines, Canada, and Australia. Also contains a discussion of methods and approaches for cross-cultural judicial behavior studies.

Frontiers of Judicial Research. Joel B. Grossman and Joseph Tanenhaus, eds. New York: John Wiley and Sons, 1969.

The presentation of papers delivered at the Shambaugh Conference held at the University of Iowa in 1967. The conference was attended by many of the leading public law scholars and represents a high point in the study of judicial behavior.

The Legal Process from a Behavioral Perspective. Stuart S. Nagel. Homewood, Ill.: The Dorsey Press, 1969.

A collection of the author's previously published articles. An excellent example of a leading public law scholar at work.

The Politics of the Bench and Bar: Judicial Selection Under the Missouri Nonpartisan Plan. Rondal G. Downing. New York: John Wiley and Sons, 1969.

A first-rate empirical study of the operation of the most popular of merit appointment plans of judicial selection. Studies bar politics, nominating commission politics, and attitudes concerning effectiveness of selected-versus-appointment plans of judicial selection.

Voting Patterns of the United States Supreme Court: Cases in Federalism, 1889–1959. John D. Sprague. Indianapolis: Bobbs-Merrill Co., 1968.

An evaluation of bloc and scalogram analyses with a view of moving toward a small-group theory of judicial voting.

Lawyers and Judges: The ABA and the Politics of Judicial Selection. Joel B. Grossman. New York: John Wiley and Sons. 1965.

A particularly fine study of the efforts of the American Bar Association to influence judicial selection.

Elements of Judicial Strategy. Walter F. Murphy. Chicago: University of Chicago Press, 1964.

The finest book ever written on the capability of the U.S. judiciary to influence public policy.

Judicial Behavior: A Reader in Theory and Research. Glendon Schubert, ed. Chicago: Rand McNally and Company, 1964.

A collection of articles placed within the editor's intellectual framework of what constitutes the proper study of judicial behavior. Contains many of the important judicial behavior articles published before 1964.

Political Behavioralism and Modern Jurisprudence. Theodore L. Becker. Chicago: Rand McNally and Company, 1964.

An excellent critique of the work of leading judicial behavior advocates, principally Glendon Schubert and Harold Speath. Author argues that judges are constrained in their behavior by perceptions of the judicial role. Presents an interesting experiment that provides prima facie evidence for the argument.

A Supreme Court Justice is Appointed. David J. Danelski. New York: Random House, 1964.

An important case study of the appointment to the Supreme Court of Pierce Butler by President Harding. Employing notions of transaction, influence, and personality, the author presents an interesting conceptual framework for understanding the appointment process.

Federal Government, 4th ed. K.C. Wheare. New York: Oxford University Press, 1963.

A thoughtful comparative analysis of federalism as a governmental system. The best work on the subject.

Federal Courts in the Political Process. Jack W. Peltason. New York: Random House, 1955.

An argument for and presentation of an interest group approach to the study of courts.

Lawyers and the Constitution. Benjamin Twiss. Princeton: Princeton University Press, 1942.

An early study recognizing the vital relationship between the bench and the bar. Demonstrates how a small elite segment of the bar had a far-reaching impact upon the development of U.S. constitutional law.

3
Footnotes and Bibliography

Few aspects of writing cause as much confusion and bewilderment as the proper use of footnotes. They are an essential part of scholarly writing, but until the fundamentals of their use are mastered, the requirement can be a constant source of frustration. As a writing device, footnotes are useful because they allow important information to be communicated without overburdening the text. More specifically, they allow a writer to reflect both credit and blame where they are due by showing the source of facts and ideas, thereby permitting the reader to utilize cited sources. In addition, footnotes act as a helpful context for presented information, indicating the sources, thus allowing the reader to judge the possible bias of such sources. Finally, they permit a writer to discuss interesting sidelights of the material without breaking the flow of writing.

Two questions invariably arise whenever footnotes are required:
1. What should be footnoted?
2. What form is correct, particularly if unusual or specialized material is being used, such as mimeographed campaign literature?

WHAT TO FOOTNOTE

Although most style manuals or term paper handbooks deal with footnote form, few ever touch upon the more difficult and confusing question of what kind of source should be footnoted and when. There are no ready answers to this question and, unfortunately, it is easy to succumb to excess in either direction. If one feels uneasy about an assignment, the material, or the professor's standards and expectations, it is tempting to "overdocument" a paper or to hang footnotes on it as though one were decorating a Christmas tree. This approach can be hazardous, for besides wasting time, the reader is overburdened with needless side trips to the bottom of the page, and the likelihood of making technical errors is increased. Such errors would, of course, detract from the substance of a paper. Unnecessary footnotes, far from being a safeguard, can become a real problem.

Equally hazardous is the practice of "underdocumentation." If footnoting has always been a mystery, something to be avoided, the possibility arises that the material will be distorted: important points may be omitted to avoid documentation. Or the source of information and ideas may be left to the reader's imagination, implying that the work of others is somehow your own.

Between these two unfortunate extremes three styles of scholarship are defined: the original scholar, the scholarly summarizer, and the essayist/journalist. The style that most closely approximates the assigned type of paper should be followed. The *original scholar form* is appropriate for Ph.D. dissertations, Master's theses, honors papers, or term papers that fulfill the major portion of the requirements for a course. This style should also be used for papers consisting mainly of scholarly research from primary sources.

The *scholarly summarizer style* is appropriate for more frequently assigned term papers that fulfill a minor portion of the requirements for a course. This type of paper usually consists of a summary, interpretation, and synthesis of secondary sources.

The *essayist/journalist style* is also appropriate for many types of term papers, but in such cases the emphasis is upon the writer's own experience or interpretation. Strictly speaking, there are few ideas that are completely new; however, if the emphasis is to be on an original and creative reaction to these ideas, and not on the ideas themselves or their origin, the essayist style is appropriate. This style may also be used if the paper is primarily a personal account or a narrative of events witnessed or situations in which the writer participated.

Table 3–1 summarizes the use of footnotes for each of the styles of scholarship.

Quotations

There is little question concerning the footnoting of direct quotations. The original scholar and the scholarly summarizer almost always footnote direct quotations. The exceptions for even the most scholarly styles are quotations from such items of public domain as the Bible and the Constitution. In such cases it is permissible to incorporate a general reference into the text of the material. Form for quotations is covered in the next section.

Example. There seemed little question that the proposal violated the "equal protection clause," the Fourteenth Amendment to the Constitution. The dogmatic insistence of the neighborhood leader's position reminded one of Henry Clay's, "Sir, I would rather be right than President."

The essayist and journalist makes even greater use of the device of incorporating general references into the body of the text.

Example. The writer as a witness or observer: "Sir," Reynaud replied, "we know that you will carry on. We would also if we saw any hope of victory." Winston S. Churchill, *Their Finest Hour, The Second World War* (Boston: Houghton Mifflin, 1949).

TABLE 3-1
THREE TYPES OF SCHOLARSHIP AND APPROPRIATE
FOOTNOTE USE

Type of Information	Original Scholar	Scholarly Summarizer	Essayist/Journalist
Quotations	All except those quotations of common knowledge, in which case they would still be footnoted if they varied from one edition to another.	Same as original scholar.	Only if the quotation is controversial or highly significant to the text, in which case the reference would be incorporated into the body of the material.
Facts 1. Controversial 2. Significant to the paper 3. Obscure	All but those that are part of common knowledge.	All controversial facts, a representative amount of significant facts to indicate the nature of sources, and only obscure facts that are central to the meaning of the paper.	Only controversial facts central to the meaning of the paper.

Facts

The original scholar footnotes all but the most obvious facts. If in doubt he asks himself if the average mature reader would automatically be aware of the origin and authenticity of a particular fact. If not, it should be footnoted. In general, the three criteria for footnoting facts are:

1. *Controversiality:* Could honest men or women disagree over the authenticity or significance of this fact?
2. *Significance to the paper:* Does a significant part of the argument rest upon this fact?
3. *Obscurity:* Are the means or sources for establishing the authenticity of this fact beyond the average reader's experience or recall? In general, if a fact could be questioned in a scholarly paper on the basis of any of these three criteria, it should be footnoted.

The scholarly summarizer needs to footnote only a representative sampling of his significant facts. In this way, the type of sources used is indicated. Obscure facts need not be footnoted unless they are central to the significance of the paper.

The essayist/journalist seldom footnotes facts unless they are both controversial and significant to the basic purpose of the paper.

Bibliography

All three styles of scholarship utilize bibliographies, but there is a slight variation between the two more scholarly styles and that of the essayist/journalist. Both the original scholar and the scholarly summarizer place their bibliographic entries in categories of written form. The most common are books, periodicals, newspapers (sometimes combined with periodicals), government documents, dissertations, unpublished manuscripts, interviews, and letters. The essayist/journalist usually does not have enough citations to justify separate categories, and simply lists all sources alphabetically, by the last name of the author. A bibliography should include all works cited in footnotes plus any other works that were used. Works that were examined but not used should not be cited.

FORM

Footnote and bibliography forms are one of the few things in life in which one can justifiably be arbitrary. There is no inherent reason to use one form rather than another, except for the sake of clear communication and consistency. The works used should be cited in the same form as that used in indexes, bibliographies, or library card catalogs. In this way, a reader will be able to locate cited sources.

Following are examples of the most frequent types of footnotes and bibliographies used in a political science paper. Those interested in employing the formal legal citation method see, the Harvard Law Review Association. *A Uniform System of Citation,* 12th ed., Cambridge, Mass.: 1976.

Footnotes, General Rules

Books should include:
1. Author's full name
2. Complete title
3. Editor, compiler, or translator (if any)
4. Name of series, volume or series number (if any)
5. Number of volumes
6. City, publisher, and date
7. Volume number and page number

Articles should include:
1. Author
2. Title of article
3. Periodical
4. Volume of periodical
5. Date and page numbers of article

Unpublished material should include:
1. Author
2. Title (if any)
3. Type of material
4. Where it may be found
5. Date
6. Page number (if any)

Bibliography, General Rules

Footnote style can be changed into bibliographic style by transposing the author's first and last names, removing parentheses from facts of publication, omitting page references, and repunctuating with periods instead of commas.

Books should include:
1. Name of author(s), editors, or institutions responsible
2. Full title, including subtitle if one exists
3. Series (if any)
4. Volume number
5. Edition, if not the original
6. Publisher's name (sometimes omitted)
7. Date of publication

Articles should include:
1. Name of author
2. Title of article
3. Name of periodical
4. Volume number (or date, or both)
5. Pages

LEGAL CITATIONS

Court Cases

When referring to a court case in the body of the text always underline the name of the case. However, for footnote and bibliographic entries it is not necessary to underline case names. Whenever possible cite the official report of the jurisdiction. For United States Supreme Court opinions the official report (U.S.) alone, without accompanying parallel citations, is usually although not always preferred.

U.S. Supreme Court
Footnote: 1. Olmstead v. United States, 277 U.S. 438 (1928).
Bibliography: Olmstead v. United States. 277 U.S. 438 (1928).

U.S. Supreme Court (Reporter's name)
Footnote: 2. Marbury v. Madison, 1 Cranch 137 (1803).
Bibliography: Marbury v. Madison. 1 Cranch 137 (1803).

Federal Reporter (Fed.)
Footnote: 3. Penn v. San Juan Hospital, Inc., 528 F. 2d 1181 (10th Cir. 1975).
Bibliography: Penn v. San Juan Hospital, Inc. 528 F. 2d 1181 (10th Cir. 1975).

Federal Supplement (F. Supp.)
Footnote: 4. Douds v. International Brotherhood, etc., 85 F. Supp. 429
          (S.D.N.Y. 1949).
Bibliography: Douds v. International Brotherhood, etc. 85 F. Supp. 429
          (S.D.N.Y. 1949).

Federal Cases (Fed. Cases)
Footnote: 5. United States v. Burr, 25 Fed. Cas. 1 (No. 14,692) (C.C. D.
          Kent. 1806).
Bibliography: United States v. Burr. 25 Fed. Cas. 1 (No. 14,692) (C.C. D.
          Kent. 1806).

Federal Rules Decisions (F.R.D.)
Footnote: 6. Tiernan v. Westext Transport, Inc., 46 F.R.D. 3 (1969).
Bibliography: Tiernan v. Westext Transport, Inc. 46 F.R.D. 3 (1969).

U.S. Law Week (USLW)
Footnote: 7. Schweiker v. Gray Panthers, 49 USLW 4792 (U.S. June 25, 1981).
Bibliography: Schweiker v. Gray Panthers. 49 USLW 4792 (U.S. June 25, 1981).

State Cases
    Cite both the official and West reports. If a state does not employ an
official reporter system or if the official reports are unavailable, cite West
report and include the state name.

Footnote: 8. People v. Savino, 44 N.Y. 2d 669, 376 N.E. 2d 196 (1978).
Bibliography: People v. Savino. 44 N.Y. 2d 669, 376 N.E. 2d 196 (1978).
Footnote: 9. Beller v. De Lara, 565 S. W. 2d 319 (Tex. 1978).
Bibliography: Beller v. De Lara. 565 S. W. 2d 319 (Tex. 1978).

Annotated Law Reports
Footnote: 10. Annot., 44 *ALR Fed* 692 (1979).
Bibliography: *American Law Reports Federal.* Vol. 44, (1979): 692–696.

Federal Statute
Footnote: 11. *Voting Rights Act of 1965, Amendments,* Pub. L. No. 94–73
          § 301, 89 Stat. 402 (1975).

Bibliography: *Voting Rights Act of 1965, Amendments.* Pub. L. No. 94–73
§ 301, 89 Stat. 402 (1975).

Federal Code
Footnote: 12. *Voting Rights Act of 1965, Amendments,* @42 U.S.C.,
@1973aa–1. (1975).
Bibliography: *Voting Rights Act of 1965, Amendments.* @42 U.S.C., @1973
aa–1. (1975).

State Code
Footnote: 13. *How Judicial Record of Foreign Country Proved,* @6 North
Dakota Century Code @ 31–09–04, (The Allen Smith Com-
pany, 1976).
Bibliography: *How Judicial Record of Foreign Country Proved.* @6 North
Dakota Century Code @ 31–09–04, The Allen Smith Company,
1976.

Federal Register (Fed. Reg.)
Footnote: 14. 46 *Fed. Reg.,* 35635 (1981).
Bibliography: *Federal Register.* Vol. 46 (1981): 35635–35637.

Code of Federal Regulations (C.F.R.)
Footnote: 15. Privacy Act Policies and Procedures, @ 22 C.F.R., @ 6.3 (1980).
Bibliography: *Privacy Act Policies and Procedures.* @ 22 C.F.R., @ 6.3 (1980).

Law Review Articles
Footnote: 16. Murray, *Mexican Criminal Jury,* 7 Ariz. L. Rev., 71 (Fall 1965).
Bibliography: Murray. *Mexican Criminal Jury.* 7 Ariz. L. Rev., Fall, 1965.

Constitution
Footnote: 17. U.S. *Const.,* Art. I, sec. 10, cl. 1.
Bibliography: U.S. *Constitution.* Article 1, section 10, clause 1.

BOOKS

Book With One Author
Footnote: 18. C. Peter Magrath, *Yazoo: Law and Politics in the New Republic*
(New York: Norton and Co., 1967), pp. 52–54.
Bibliography: Magrath, C. Peter. *Yazoo: Law and Politics in the New Republic.*
New York: Norton and Co., 1967.

Book With Two Authors
Footnote: 19. Henry Robert Glick and Kenneth N. Vines, *State Court Systems*
(Englewood Cliffs, New Jersey: Prentice-Hall, Inc., 1973), p. 17.

Bibliography: Glick, Henry Robert and Vines, Kenneth N. *State Court Systems.* Englewood Cliffs, New Jersey: Prentice-Hall, Inc., 1973.

Book With Three Authors

Footnote: 20. John E. Nowak, Ronald D. Rotunda, and J. Nelson Young, *Handbook on Constitutional Law* (St. Paul, Minn.: West Publishing Co., 1978), p. 251.

Bibliography: Nowark, John E.; Rotunda, Ronald D.; and Young, Nelson J. *Handbook on Constitutional Law.* St. Paul, Minn.: West Publishing Co., 1978.

Book With More Than Three Authors

Footnote: 21. Carl A. Auerbach et al., *The Legal Process: An Introduction to Decision-Making by Judicial, Legislative, Executive, and Administrative Agencies* (Scranton, Pennsylvania: Chandler Publishing Company, 1961), p. 507.

Bibliography: Auerbach, Carl A.; Garrison, Lloyd K.; Hurst, Willard; and Mermin, Samuel. *The Legal Process: An Introduction to Decision-Making by Judicial, Legislative, Executive, and Administrative Agencies.* Scranton, Pennsylvania: Chandler Publishing Company, 1961.

Book In A Series

Footnote: 22. Jonathan D. Casper, *The Politics of Civil Liberties,* Harper's American Political Behavior Series (New York: Harper and Row, Publishers, 1972), p. 171.

Bibliography: Casper, Jonathan D. *The Politics of Civil Liberties.* Harper's American Political Behavior Series. New York: Harper and Row, Publishers, 1972.

Book By Editor Or Translator: Author
Editors

Footnote: 23. David F. Forte, ed., *The Supreme Court in American Politics: Judicial Activism vs. Judicial Restraint* (Lexington, Mass.: D.C. Heath and Company, 1972), p. 23.

Bibliography: Forte, David F., ed. *The Supreme Court in American Politics: Judicial Activism vs. Judicial Restraint.* Lexington, Mass.: D.C. Heath and Company, 1972.

Translators

Footnote: 24. Marcus Tullius Cicero, *Laws,* trans. C. W. Keyes (Cambridge, Mass.: Harvard University Press, 1928), p. 57.

Bibliography: Cicero, Marcus Tullius, *Laws.* Translated by C. W. Keyes. Cambridge, Mass.: Harvard University Press, 1928.

Book, Multivolume
Footnote: 25. Paul C. Bartholomew, *American Constitutional Law,* 2 vols.
(Totowa, New Jersey: Littlefield, Adams and Company, 1978),
1: 68.
Bibliography: Bartholomew, Paul C. *American Constitutional Law.* Vol. 1
Totowa, New Jersey: Littlefield, Adams and Company, 1978.

Citation in One Book from Another Book
Footnote: 26. Charles Warren, *The Supreme Court in United States History,*
vol. 2, p. 138. As quoted in John R. Schmidhauser, *Judges
and Justices: The Federal Appellate Judiciary* (Boston: Little,
Brown and Company, 1979), p. 141.
Bibliography: Schmidhauser, John R. *Judges and Justices: The Federal Appellate Judiciary.* Boston: Little, Brown and Company, 1979.

Book Review
Footnote: 27. Robert H. Birkby, "American Politics," Review of *The Wall of
Separation: The Constitutional Politics of Church and State,*
by Frank J. Sorauf, *American Political Science Review* 72 (March
1978): 285.
Bibliography: Birkby, Robert H. "American Politics." Review of *The Wall
of Separation: The Constitutional Politics of Church and State,*
by Frank J. Sorauf. *American Political Science Review* 72 (March
1978): 285–286.

Classical Works
Footnote: 28. Julius Caesar, *The Conquest of Gaul* 1., 2–4.
Bibliography: Caesar, Julius. *The Conquest of Gaul* 1.

Modern Edition of Classical Work
Footnote: 29. Aristotle, *Politics and Poetics,* trans. Benjamin Jowett and
Thomas Twining 2. 25.
Bibliography: Aristotle. *Politics and Poetics.* Translated by Benjamin Jowett
and Thomas Twining.

Book In a Series, One Author, Several Volumes, Each With a Different Title
Footnote: 30. Richard H. Maloy, *Your Questions Answered About Florida
Law* & *Family Relationships in Life* & *Death,* 3 vols., Your Ques-
tions Answered on Florida Law Series (Miami, Florida: Wind-
ward Publishing, 1978), 2:32.
Bibliography: Maloy, Richard H. *Your Questions Answered About Florida Law
& Family Relationships in Life* & *Death.* Vol. 2. Your Questions
Answered on Florida Law Series. Miami, Florida: Windward
Publishing, 1978.

Paperback Edition of Book First Published in Hard Cover
Footnote: 31. Willard Gaylin, *Partial Justice: A Study of Bias in Sentencing*
                (New York: Vintage Books, paperback, 1975), p. 95.
Bibliography: Gaylin, Willard. *Partial Justice: A Study of Bias in Sentencing*.
                Paperback. New York: Vintage Books, 1975.

Introduction or Foreword to Book by Another Author
Footnote: 32. Harry S. Young, Foreword to *The Unforgettables,* by Judge
                Wallace L. Ware (Hertford, England: Mimram Press, 1965),
                p.82.
Bibliography: Young, Harry S. Foreword to *The Unforgettables,* by Judge
                Wallace L. Ware. Hertford, England: Mimram Press, 1965.

Book With an Association As Author
Footnote: 33. Association of Law Schools, the Law School Admission Council,
                and Educational Testing Service, *Pre Law Hand Book* (Prince-
                ton, N.J.: Law School Admission Services, 1976), p. 29.
Bibliography: Association of Law Schools, the Law School Admission Council,
                and Educational Testing Service. *Pre Law Hand Book*. Prince-
                ton, N.J.: Educational Testing Service, 1976.

Author's Name Not on Title Page, but Known
Footnote: 34. [Alexander Hamilton, James Madison, and John Jay] *The
                Federalist* (New York: The Modern Library, 1941), p. 53.
Bibliography: [Hamilton, Alexander; Madison, James; and Jay, John.] *The
                Federalist*. New York: The Modern Library, 1941.

Article, Chapter, or Other Part of a Book
Footnote: 35. Alexander Meiklejohn, "The Rulers and the Ruled," *The
                Principles and Practices of Freedom of Speech,* edited by Haig
                A. Bosmajian (New York: Houghton Mifflin Company, 1971),
                p. 303.
Bibliography: Meiklejohn, Alexander. "The Rulers and the Ruled," *The Prin-
                ciples and Practices of Freedom of Speech*. Edited by Haig A.
                Bosmajian. New York: Houghton Mifflin Company, 1971.

Pseudonym, Author's Real Name Known
Footnote: 36. George Tichnor Curtis [Peter Boylston], *The Constitutional
                History of the United States, From the Declaration of Indepen-
                dence to the Close of Their Civil War* (New York: Harper and
                Brothers, 1889), p. 31.
Bibliography: Curtis, George Tichnor [Peter Boylston]. *The Constitutional
                History of the United States, From the Declaration of Indepen-
                dence to the Close of Their Civil War*. New York: Harper and
                Brothers, 1889.

Book's Author Anonymous
Footnote: 37. *A Constitution of the United States of America . . . By a Citizen* (Washington, D.C.: Printed by J. and G. S. Gideon, 1846), p. 5.
Bibliography: *A Constitution of the United States of America . . . By a Citizen.* Washington, D.C.: Printed by J. and G.S. Gideon, 1846.
Comments: Avoid use of "Anon." or "Anonymous."

LITERATURE

Plays and Long Poems
Footnote: 38. Maxwell Anderson, *Winterset,* act 2, sc. 1, lines 5–19.
Bibliography: Anderson, Maxwell. *Winterset.*

Short Poems
Footnote: 39. Rod McKuen, "Did You Say the War is Over?" *In Someone's Shadow* (New York: Cheval Books, 1969), lines 8–9.
Bibliography: McKuen, Rod. "Did You Say the War is Over?" *In Someone's Shadow.* New York: Cheval Books, 1969.

Bible
Footnote: 40. 13 Romans 2:7.
Bibliography: The Bible.

PERIODICALS

Periodical: Author Given
Footnote: 41. Elliot E. Slotnick, "The Chief Justices and Self-Assignment of Majority Opinions: A Research Note," *The Western Political Quarterly* XXXI (June 1978): 219.
Bibliography: Slotnick, Elliot E. "The Chief Justices and Self-Assignment of Majority Opinions: A Research Note." *The Western Political Quarterly* XXXI (June 1978): 219–225.

Magazine Article, No Author Given
Footnote: 42. "Rough Justice in Mississippi," *Time,* 26 February 1979, p. 49.
Bibliography: "Rough Justice in Mississippi." *Time,* 26 February 1979, p. 49.

NEWSPAPERS

American
Footnote: 43. "Court Mandates No Segregation of the Retarded," *The New York Times,* 1 March 1979, p. A 20.

Bibliography: "Court Mandates No Segregation of the Retarded." *The New York Times*, 1 March 1979, p. A 20.

Comment: When author byline is presented name author at beginning of citation.

Foreign
Footnote: 44. *Times* (London), 5 December 1981, p. 4.
Bibliography: *Times*. London. 5 December 1981, p. 4.
Comments: Include name of city for foreign newspapers.

ENCYCLOPEDIAS, ALMANACS, AND OTHER REFERENCE WORKS

Signed Articles
Footnote: 45. *International Encyclopedia of the Social Sciences*, Vol. 3, 1968, s.v. "Constitutional Law," by C. Herman Pritchett, pp. 295–300.
Bibliography: *International Encyclopedia of the Social Sciences*. Vol. 3, 1968, s.v. "Constitutional Law," by C. Herman Pritchett.

Unsigned Articles
Footnote: 46. *The World Almanac & Book of Facts 1981*, s.v. "The Federal Judicial System," p. 825.
Bibliography: *The World Almanac & Book of Facts 1981*. s.v. "The Federal Judicial System."

Legal Encyclopedias
Footnote: 47. 16 Am. Jur. 2d, "Constitutional Law" § 17 (1979), p. 329.
Bibliography: *American Jurisprudence 2d*, vol. 16, 1979, "Constitutional Law" § 17.
Footnote: 48. 36 C.J.S., "Federal Courts," § 42 (1960), p. 233.
Bibliography: *Corpus Juris Secundum*, vol. 36, 1960, "Federal Courts" § 42

Material from Manuscript Collections
Footnote: 49. Administration of Justice and Courts, 1916—, Richard Richards Papers, Library of University of California, Los Angeles, Los Angeles, California, p. 6.
Bibliography: Los Angeles, California. Library of University of California, Los Angeles, Administration of Justices and Courts, 1916—. Richard Richards Papers.

Radio and Television Programs
Footnote: 50. CBS, *CBS Evening News*, 7 December 1976, "Death Penalty," Fred Graham, reporter.

Bibliography: CSB. *CBS Evening News.* 7 December 1976. "Death Penalty."
Fred Graham, reporter.

Interview
Footnote: 51. Interview with Mr. Carl Rauh, Deputy Attorney General for
the District of Columbia, Washington, D.C., December 2,
1970.
Bibliography: Interview with Mr. Carl Rauh, Deputy Attorney General for the
District of Columbia. Washington, D.C., December 2, 1970.

Mimeographed or Other Nonprinted Reports
Footnote: 52. Boyd L. Wright and Lloyd A. Bakken, "North Dakota Constitutional Convention Delegates," mimeographed (Grand Forks,
N.D.: Bureau of Governmental Affairs, University of North
Dakota, January, 1971), p. 29.
Bibliography: Wright, Boyd L. and Bakken, Lloyd A. "North Dakota Constitutional Convention Delegates." Grand Forks, N.D.: Bureau
of Governmental Affairs, University of North Dakota, January,
1971.

Pamphlet
Footnote: 53. 1972 North Dakota Constitutional Convention, "Framing the
Basic Document," (Bismarck, North Dakota, 1972), p. 2.
Bibliography: 1972 North Dakota Constitutional Convention. "Framing the
Basic Document." Bismarck, North Dakota, 1972.

Proceedings of a Meeting or Conference: Reproduced
Footnote: 54. Annual Report of the American Bar Association Including
Proceedings of the Ninety-Seventh Annual Meeting, "Informa-
tional Report of the Section of Individual Rights and Responsibilities," (Honolulu, Hawaii: August 12–16, 1974), p. 1054.
Bibliography: Annual Report of the American Bar Association Including
Proceedings of the Ninety-Seventh Annual Meeting, "Informa-
tional Report of the Section of Individual Rights and Responsibilities." Honolulu, Hawaii: August 12–16, 1974.

Paper Read or Speech Delivered at a Meeting
Footnote: 55. Kenneth A. Wagner, "Avenues of Legal Profession Influence
on Public Attitudes Toward Courts" (Paper delivered at the
1973 Meetings of the Western Political Science Association, San
Diego, California, April 5–7, 1973), p. 12.
Bibliography: Wagner, Kenneth A. "Avenues of Legal Profession Influence
on Public Attitudes Toward Courts." Paper delivered at the
1973 Meetings of the Western Political Science Association,
April 5–7, 1973, at San Diego, California.

Thesis or Dissertation
Footnote: 56. Ruben Julian Vega, "The Controversy over the Constitutional
                Authority of Government Eavesdropping" (M.A. Thesis, Cali-
                fornia State University, Long Beach, 1974), p. 179.
Bibliography: Vega, Ruben Julian. "The Controversy over the Constitutional
                Authority of Government Eavesdropping." M.A. Thesis, Cali-
                fornia State University, Long Beach, 1974.

DOCUMENTS

Citing documents is always a difficult problem, for their form is totally
unlike that of books and magazines. The card catalog is a good guide, and the
following general rules should help. Include, in this order:

1. The country (U.S., etc.)
2. The branch of government (legislative, executive, etc.)
3. The subbranch or subbranches (House, Committee on Education and
   Labor, etc.)

The branches or subbranches can become complicated, but a careful examination of the document itself, its entry in the card catalog, or the *Government
Organization Manual* should give an idea as to the sequence of organization.

This information is followed by the title (underlined), the name of the
series or sequence, and the facts of publication. The following examples
include the most commonly cited government publications.

Congressional Documents

Bills
Footnote: 57. U.S., Congress, House, *Privacy Act of 1977,* H.R. 6258, 95th
                Cong., 1st sess., 1977.
Bibliography: U.S. Congress. House. *Privacy Act of 1977.* H.R. 6258, 95th
                Cong., 1st sess., 1977.
Footnote: 58. U.S., Congress, Senate, *Speedy Trial Act of 1974,* S. 754, 93rd
                Cong., 2nd sess., 1974.
Bibliography: U.S. Congress. Senate. *Speedy Trial Act of 1974.* S. 754, 93rd
                Cong., 2nd sess., 1974.

Debates
Footnotes: 59. U.S., Congress, House, *Congressional Record,* 90th Cong.,
                 2nd sess., 1968, pt. 12: 1538.
Bibliography: U.S. Congress. House. *Congressional Record.* 90th Congress,
                2nd sess., 1968. 12: 1538.

Report
Footnote: 60. U.S., Congress, House, *Privacy Act of 1977,* H. Rept. 342 to
                Accompany H. R. 6258, 95th Cong., 1st sess., 1977.

Bibliography: U.S. Congress. House. *Privacy Act of 1977*. H.R. 6258. 95th
Cong., 1st sess., 1977.

Hearings
Footnote: 61. U.S., Congress, House, Committee on Judiciary, Hearings to
offer newsmen and publishers limited protection from compulsory disclosure of news sources and conformation in Federal
and State Courts, H.R. 215, 94th Cong., 1st sess., 1975.
Bibliography: U.S. Congress. House. Committee on Judiciary. Hearings to
offer newsmen and publishers limited protection from compulsory disclosure of news sources and information in Federal and
State Courts, H.R. 215. 94th Cong., 1st sess., 1975.

Executive Documents

From an Executive Department
Footnote: 62. U.S., Department of Commerce, *1977 Census of Governments:
"Governmental Organization"* vol. 1, no. 1 (Washington,
D.C.: U.S. Department of Commerce, Bureau of the Census,
1977), p. 25.
Bibliography: U.S. Department of Commerce. *1977 Census of Government:*
"Governmental Organization." Vol. 1, no. 1. Washington,
D.C.: U.S. Department of Commerce, Bureau of the Census,
1977.

Presidential Papers
Footnote: 63. U.S. President, "Statement on Signing H.R. 7843 Into Law,
October 20, 1978," *Weekly Compilation of Presidential Docu-
ments,* vol. 14, no. 42, October 23, 1978, p. 1803.
Bibliography: U.S. President. "Statement on Signing H.R. 7843 Into Law,
October 20, 1978." *Weekly Compilation of Presidential Docu-
ments.* October 23, 1978.

International Documents

International Organizations
Footnote: 64. Organization of American States, *Report of the OAS to the
International Conference on Human Rights, 1968* OEA/Ser.L/
V/1.5 December 18, 1967, p. 41.
Bibliography: Organization of American States. *Report of the OAS to the
International Conference on Human Rights, 1968* OEA/Ser.L./
V/1.5, December 18, 1967.

Treaties
Footnote: 65. *U.S. Statutes at Large* 43, pt. 2 (December 1923–March 1925),
"Naval Arms Limitation Treaty," February 26, 1922, ch. 1,
art. 1, p. 1655.

Bibliography: U.S. Statutes at Large 43, pt. 2 (December 1923–March 1925). "Naval Arms Limitation Treaty." February 26, 1922.

State and Local Documents

State
Footnote: 66. William G. Bohn, *North Dakota Courtrooms,* 1975 (Bismarck, N.D.: The North Dakota Supreme Court, 1976), p. 53.
Bibliography: Bohn, William G. *North Dakota Courtrooms, 1975.* Bismarck, N.D.: North Dakota Supreme Court, 1976.

City
Footnote: 67. New York, N.Y., Mayor's Office, Mayor's Task Force on Reorganization of New York City Government, *The Mayor's Task Force on Reorganization of New York City Government: Report and Proposed Local Law* (New York: Institute of Public Administration, 1966), p. 9.
Bibliography: New York, N.Y. Mayor's Office. Mayor's Task Force on Reorganization of New York City Government. *The Mayor's Task Force on Reorganization of New York City Government: Report and Proposed Local Law.* New York: Institute of Public Administration, 1966.

SECOND OR LATER REFERENCES TO FOOTNOTES

Chances are that several references wil be made to the same footnote. The general rules are as follows:

1. For references to the same work with no intervening footnotes simply use the Latin term "Ibid.," meaning "in the same place."
2. For second references with no intervening footnote, but with a different page of the same work, state Ibid. and the page number. Example: Ibid., p. 87.
3. For second references with intervening footnotes, state: the author's last name, but not first name or initials unless another author of the same name is cited; a shortened title of the work; and the specific page number.

Following are examples of second citations of a representative number of works.

Second References with Intervening Citations

Book, Single Volume
First Citation: 1. Lawrence Baum, *The Supreme Court* (Washington, D.C.: Congressional Quarterly Press, 1981), p. 75.
Second Citation: 8. Baum, *The Supreme Court,* p. 137.

Multivolume
First Citation: 2. R.W. Carlyle, and A.D. Carlyle, *A History of Medieval Political Law in the West,* 6 vols. (London: Charles Black, 1903–1936) 1:5.
Second Citation: 9. Carlyle and Carlyle, *A History of Medieval Political Law in the West,* 1:8.

Journal Article
First Citation: 3. Sallie Fisher, "The Legacy of John Marshall," *Journal of Politics* 54 (1979): 168.
Second Citation: 8. Fisher, "The Legacy of John Marshall," p. 168.

Classical
First Citation: 4. Thucydides, *History of the Peloponnesian Wars,* 2.30, 1.
Second Citation: 9. Thucy., 2.28, 1–6.

Letters
First Citation: 5. Stevens to Sumner, 28 August 1865, Charles Sumner Papers, Harvard College Library, Cambridge, Mass.
Second Citation: 14. Stevens to Sumner, 28 August 1865.

State Documents
First Citation: 6. Ohio, *Ordinance Number 438,* (1982) sec.8.
Second Citation: 15. Ohio, *Ordinance Number 438,* sec. 8.

Federal Documents
First Citation: 7. U.S., *Statutes at Large 43,* pt. 2 (Dec. 1923–March 1925), "Naval Arms Limitation Treaty," Feb. 26, 1922, ch. 1, art. 1, p. 1655.
Second Citation: 16. U.S., *Statutes at Large 43,* "Naval Arms Limitation Treaty," p. 1655.

Court Case
First Citation: 8. Olmstead v. United States, 277 U.S. 438 (1928).
Second Citation: 26. 277 U.S. at 440. Or 277 US. 438, 440.

4

Why And How To Brief
a Case

Briefing a case means reducing the written opinion of a court to its most basic and essential elements. Typically, full opinions of reported cases are many printed pages long. Editors of instructional casebooks then reduce the full opinions to those parts of the cases they believe are most relevant. Although editors occasionally will summarize the facts of the case, they typically do not change the exact words of the opinion. Rather they simply delete those words, sentences, paragraphs, or sections they regard as not particularly instructive. Occasionally, an instructor will send students to the library to read and brief a case from the full reported opinion of a court. Most often however, instructors will ask students to brief cases which have been edited and placed in a course-required casebook. The result is that much of the analysis of the case is already completed by the editor and the student need only to further reduce the opinion to its bare bones.

For some students the mere mention of putting ideas to paper precipitates an immediate exit from the class. Others do not believe that the instructor is really serious and will wait for the drop date before exiting. Those who remain may complain that the requirement or suggestion to prepare briefs requires too much preparation time and other important courses must suffer as a result. Consequently, a justification for briefing cases is in order.

Briefing cases serves five related purposes. First, the number of cases discussed in a typical constitutional law course is impossible to recall from the memory of one or two readings. Opinions are usually complicated and the numbers are too great. By writing down the essential elements of the case, the information can be firmly implanted in the student mind.

Second, briefs are an excellent study tool when preparing for examinations. Attempting to read, comprehend and remember constitutional law materials for the first time the night before a scheduled examination inevitably meets with academic disaster. If the student reads and briefs the cases as the course progresses, he or she can then sit down before an examination and review the cases, making the connections required to see the forest through the many trees. This is, at any rate, the best formula for success.

Third, reading and briefing cases provides one dominant method for understanding how the law develops. The growth of the law is traced through a series of cases; the earlier cases serve as the precedent and foundation for present cases. By observing the intimate relationship between the facts and decisions of past and present cases, the student gains an appreciation for the historical method of the common law. In most law schools, this case-method approach is exalted as the best way to train lawyers. This contention has been hotly debated as tending to blind students to extra-legal material relevant to policymaking. Political scientists are alert to this problem. Yet it is desirable to employ at least some aspects of the case-method approach for at least two reasons. (A) It is necessary to know what the courts have said. The courts make policy and it is important to know precisely what the policy is. Reading the primary and authoritative source material of judicial policymaking, the written opinion, the confusion, misinformation and improper interpretation often detected in public debate can be avoided. And, (B) as students of politics, it is important to understand the workings of the legal mind and this can best be accomplished by studying lawyers and judges on their own terms. To be sure, the terms are often narrow and confining. But unlike law students and working attorneys, a clear understanding of the cases is not the end of analysis; for political scientists it is the beginning. So it is a necessary task for political scientists to learn what the law is and then to explain why the decisions were made the way they were, how the cases reflect values in and out of courts, and the public policy consequences of adjudication. In short, it is not the goal of political scientists to make constitutional lawyers out of undergraduates. The goal is to understand when, how, and why the law influences the allocation of authority within the political system.

The fourth justification for briefing cases is that it provides students and teacher with a common point of departure for the discussion of meaningful problems. Possessing a common text, one in which real people are in actual conflict, a class is in the position to discuss not only what might appear to be mundane legal issues, but also the often dramatic implications of decisions for government and society. Touching almost all aspects of social science and the humanities, the student comes to appreciate the interdisciplinary nature of the subject matter. In such a setting, the synthesis of ideas can occur and often does.

The last justification for briefing cases is the lasting value of disciplined thinking. Long after the cases are but dim recollections, the experience of rigorous reading and writing will endure. The careful and thoughtful process necessary for writing briefs introduces an appreciation for critical thinking and prepares one to deal with future challenges. In this sense, a rigorous constitutional law course is among the very best liberal arts courses offered on college campuses. It trains the mind to be alert and requires carefully written analysis of real life problems in the political system.

ELEMENTS OF A BRIEF

Below is a listing and discussion of the elements of a brief. A model brief is also provided. It should be noted that there is no accepted standard for brief writing. Instructors often have their own recommendations for the desired form. Yet our presentation is fairly consistent with most recommendations. It must be emphasized that a brief should be just that, brief! Moreover, the writer should make every effort to put the brief in his or her own words.

I. *Name or Title of Case.* This should appear at the top of the page.

II. *Legal Citation.* The citation of a case is the location in court reports where full reported opinions of the case may be found. Usually a single citation will suffice; *e.g.,* 392 U.S. 409 (1968). The parallel citations could also be included at the option of the student; *e.g.,* 392 U.S. 409, 20 L.Ed. 2d 1189, 88 S.Ct. 2186 (1968). If at some later point in time it becomes desirable to read the full reported opinion, knowledge of its location will ease the library search.

III. *Statement of Facts.* The facts include the circumstances of the dispute giving rise to the lawsuit. But for purposes of a brief, only those facts treated by the author of the opinion as relevant and those facts specifically treated as irrelevant should be included in the written brief. Usually, the facts appear at the beginning of the written opinion. Unfortunately however, this is not always the case. It is sometimes necessary to search the majority, and on occasion the concurring and dissenting opinions, for the facts. The statement of facts should also include the decisions and actions of the lower courts and how the case came before the Supreme Court; *e.g.:* on appeal; certiorari; certification.

Because the object of the brief is to condense the opinion of the court, the brief writer should make every effort to put the facts in his or her own words. This is not always possible, but it should always be attempted. When phrases are lifted from any part of the opinion, use identifying quotation marks.

IV. *Statement of Issues.* An issue is a statement of the legal or constitutional question facing the court for resolution. It is not uncommon for a constitutional law case to have more than one issue. Sometimes, the court must answer affirmatively one issue before it can or needs to answer following issues. It should also be noted that editors of instructional casebooks will often delete sections of a case which are deemed unimportant. Students should be aware of this fact since often one reads about a case in one context and may be surprised that the case stands for much more in another.

Often authors of majority opinions will place the statement of the issues in one clearly identifiable place within the text of the opinion—usually immediately following the recitation of the facts of the case. However, like the facts, the issues are sometimes scattered through the entire written opinion. It is therefore important to analyze the full text before noting the issues.

Two rules should be followed when stating the issues: (1) the statement of the issue(s) should be put in the form of a question; and (2) the issues should be stated in a precise and specific manner. A case always involves answering some specific legal or constitutional question. The Supreme Court does not deal with hypothetical or general issues—the statement of issues should reflect this fact. For example, it is insufficient to write for the case of *Jones* v. *Alfred H. Mayer Company:* "May a seller of property refuse to sell to a black buyer?" Note that no legal or constitutional issue is raised and that the question is general—it deals with sellers and black buyers, not specific people with an actual controversy in law or in equity.

A proper statement of the issues is very important since it reflects an understanding of the facts, conditions the legal decision and, significantly, the reasoning of the court. Careful wording of the issues may often produce long conditional interrogative sentences. But this is all right. Given the nature of the facts, statutes or constitutional provisions such sentences are often necessary because they admit of no other useful alternative. In any event, always write the issues so that they can be clearly understood. At times, copying the issue(s) as stated by the court is the best format. However, whenever possible, put the issues in one's own words, making sure to keep those vital words or phrases of the opinion that are indispensable to understanding.

V. *Decision and Action.* For the decision simply provide a *yes* or *no* answer. No explanation is required at this point. The action of the court will usually appear at the end of the court's written opinion. It directs that something should be done; *e.g.,* case reversed, or reversed and remanded, or affirmed and other possibilities.

VI. *Reasoning of the Court.* The reasons for the court's decision is the heart of the opinion. The reasoning contains the court's attempt to justify its decision in the case. But not everything written may be relevant for the purposes of the brief. Only that part of the reasoning which is directly supportive of the decision is appropriate for inclusion in the brief. There is often argument which is not directly related to the issues and decision in the case. This verbiage is usually referred to as obiter dicta, or simply obiter, or dicta, or dictum. It is, so to speak, excess intellectual baggage—argument unnecessary for the court to logically come to its decision in the case.

Given the basic objective of a brief it is necessary to read the court's opinion carefully, separating those reasons which are essential for the decision and those which are not. The key to separating the wheat from the chaff is the statement of the issues. Only those arguments necessary for supporting the answers to the issues should be part of the brief. Obviously, this task requires careful reading and analysis. At first, novice brief writers will encounter difficulties. With experience this artful task becomes easier.

On the first line of this section of the brief note the author of the court's opinion; *e.g.,* Per Stewart. It is also wise to number the reasoning consistent with each statement of the issues. This permits quick eye movement between the issues, decision and reasoning.

VII. *Concurring Opinion(s).* A concurring opinion is one that agrees with the result of the majority decision but disagrees with the reasons. ("The right deed for the wrong reason,'' as one poet has put it.) Note the justice(s) writing such an opinion and briefly state his reason for the disagreement.

VIII. *Dissenting Opinion(s).* A dissenting opinion is one in which there is disagreement with the court's judgment both in terms of the result and the reasoning. Note the justice(s) writing such an opinion and his reason for disagreement.

IX. *Voting Coalition.* If the information is available, note those justices voting together. This information is of interest when examining the politics of decisionmaking.

X. *Summary of Legal Principle(s).* Briefly summarize the legal principles the case might stand for. This is a good method for pulling the elements of the case together and is a valuable study aid when preparing for examinations. Also note how the case might differ from previously studied cases on the same topic.

XI. *Free Space.* Sometimes during class discussion the flaws in one's own brief become apparent. Leaving room at the end of the brief for revision comments is an efficient way to note needed changes. Classroom comments on the case might also be placed in this space. Some students might prefer even to use a separate notebook for such purposes.

MODEL BRIEF

I.   Jones v. Alfred H. Mayer Co.

II. 392 U.S. 409, 20 L.Ed. 2d 1189, 88 S.Ct. 2186 (1968)

III. *Facts:* Joseph Jones, a black, sued for injunctive relief alleging that solely because of his race the Alfred H. Mayer Company refused to sell him a home in a St. Louis County community. Jones argued that an 1866 federal civil rights statute prohibits all such discrimination, private as well as state action. The Federal District Court dismissed the complaint and the Court of Appeals affirmed holding that the statute applied only to state and not private refusals to sell real property. On a writ of certiorari, Jones appealed to the U.S. Supreme Court.

IV. *Issues:* (1) When it enacted the 1866 Civil Rights statute, did Congress intend to prohibit all racial discrimination—whether by private parties or by state governments?

     (2) If Congress intended to cover ''private'' discrimination, is the statute a valid exercise of congressional power under the enforcement provision of the 13th Amendment?

V.   *Decision and Action:* (1) Yes; (2) Yes; Judgment Reversed.

VI. *Reasoning:* Per Stewart. (1) The plain language of the 1866 statute unambiguously grants to all citizens ''without regard to race or color, 'the same right' to purchase or lease property as is enjoyed by white citizens.'' After reviewing the legislative history of the 1866 act, the Court concluded that the Congress intended exactly what it said.

(2) It has not and cannot be denied that the power vested in the enforcement provision of the 13th Amendment includes the ability to make laws that operate directly upon individuals whether or not sanctioned by state legislation. It is a rational exercise of congressional power to determine, and translate into effective legislation, what are the badges and incidents of slavery. To purchase property is an essential requisite to civil freedom; without such an interpretation the 13th Amendment is nothing but so many words.

VII.   *Concurring Opinion:* Per Douglas.

Douglas emphasized the plight of black Americans in all areas of life. He rejects the suggestion by the majority that an argument might be made that the discrimination suffered by Jones may not be part of the customary pattern of discrimination.

VIII. *Dissenting Opinion:* Per Harlan joined by White.

Because the Civil Rights Act of 1968 is about to become operable and since it provides for relief of persons similarly situated as Jones, certiorari should be dismissed as improvidently granted. Moreover, the Court's previous precedents, including the famous *Civil Rights Cases,* have established that the 1866 Act was not intended to cover private action, only state action.

IX.   *Voting Coalitions:* For the majority, Stewart, Warren, Black, Brennan, Fortas, Marshall. Concurring, Douglas. Dissenting, Harlan and White.

X.   Summary: "Private" discrimination can be controlled by Congress under the enforcement provisions of the 13th Amendment. This case effectively overrules the *Civil Rights Cases.*

XI.   *Free Space:* (Leave approximately one-third of a page for comments.)

5

Glossary of Terms and Phrases

ABROGATE. The repeal, annulment, or destruction of an order or rule of a lower power by the same or higher authority.

ACCUSATORIAL SYSTEM. The legal system which presumes that a person is innocent until proven guilty. The outstanding feature of Anglo-American criminal justice placing the burden of proof upon the government.

AD HOC. For a special or one time purpose; temporary and not permanent.

ADJECTIVE LAW. Generic term referring to rules under which courts or agencies conduct their affairs; procedural as opposed to substantive law.

ADMINISTRATIVE LAW. The growing branch of public law dealing with the rules and regulations promulgated by government agencies.

ADMIRALTY LAW. The branch of the law concerned with maritime matters.

AD VALOREM. Latin meaning according to value. An *ad valorem* tax is a levy on the value of something rather than a fixed tax regardless of value. For example, an *ad valorem* tax on a diamond ring worth $100 might be $5 while the tax on a $10,000 ring might be $250. The tax varies according to the worth or value of the item rather than a fixed tax of, say, $75 for all diamond rings.

ADVISORY OPINION. A judicial ruling in the absence of an actual case or controversy; a ruling in a hypothetical case without bona fide litigants.

AGENCY. (A) A relationship in which one party acts on behalf of another; the former is authorized by the latter. (B) May refer to an administrative body of government.

AMICUS CURIAE. Latin meaning friend of the court. Normally an outside interest not directly a party to the suit. Usually presents a brief that provides information and argument relevant to a court in its deliberation as to matters of law.

ANALYTICAL JURISPRUDENCE. A school of jurisprudence that attempts to systematize the law utilizing tools of logic. Outstanding proponents include Hans Kelsen, John Austin, and H.L.A. Hart.

ANSWER. Usually a written statement or pleading by the defendant responding to the plaintiff's charges.

APPEAL. A generic term referring to the movement of court proceedings from an inferior to a superior court. Depending upon context, the term may refer to a technical method of moving a case to a superior court.

APPELLANT. The party who takes his or her case from a lower court to a superior court to seek review of the lower court decision.

APPELLATE COURT. A court possessing the authority to review and sustain or reverse the decisions of lower courts.

APPELLEE. The party in a suit against whom the appeal to a superior court is taken; the party with an interest in sustaining the lower court judgment.

ARBITRATION. A third party hearing and settlement of a dispute among contending parties. The decision of the arbitrator(s) may be binding upon the participants.

ARGUENTO. During the course of argument making the assumption that a statement or fact is true, although it may be true or false. A method of illustrating a line of reasoning found in many judicial opinions.

ARRAIGNMENT. The formal court procedure in which a criminal defendant answers an indictment with a plea of guilty, not guilty, or nolo contendere.

ASSOCIATE JUSTICE. The title given to judges of an appellate court excluding the chief justice.

ASSUMPSIT. From the law of contracts meaning to undertake the performance of an oral agreement. At common law assumpsit was an action taken to enforce a promise.

BAIL. The security given in the form of cash or a bail bond as a guarantee that a released prisoner will appear at his or her trial. Bail may be forfeited if the released prisoner does not appear at trial.

BAILIFF. An officer of the court who is in charge of prisoners and who guards the jurors in a court; generally charged with keeping the peace in court.

BANKRUPTCY. A legal procedure under federal law by which a person is relieved of all debts after placing all property under the court's authority. An organization may be reorganized or terminated by the court in order to pay off creditors.

BAR. The community of attorneys permitted to practice law in a particular jurisdiction or court.

BARRISTERS. The segment of the English legal profession which conducts court trials.

BICAMERAL. Two chambers. Usually refers to a legislative body with two "houses;" *e.g.,* a Senate and a House of Representatives.

BILL OF ATTAINDER. A legislative act declaring a person guilty of a crime and passing sentence without the benefit of a trial. Such legislation is specifically forbidden by the U.S. Constitution.

BLACK LETTER LAW. Refers to the most basic principle of law accepted by the courts. For example, "obscenity is not protected speech." Generally rejected by political scientists and others as not explanatory of the judicial process.

BLACKSTONE. Influential eighteenth century jurist. Author of *Blackstone's Commentaries on the Common Law.* Sir William Blackstone.

BLUE LAW. Legislative enactment forbidding all or certain business activity on Sundays.

BONA FIDE. Latin for good faith. A term referring to acting in good faith; without trickery, deceit, fraud, or dishonesty.

BRANDEIS BRIEF. A written argument presented before an appellate court containing extralegal social science information relevant to the case. Named after Louis Brandeis whose brief in *Muller v. Oregon* 208 U.S. 412(1908) consisted of two pages of formal legal argument and 100 pages of economic and social data.

BREACH OF CONTRACT. The nonperformance of the terms of a legally binding oral or written agreement.

BRIEF. (A) The oral or written argument presented by counsel to a court. (B) A summary of the pertinent elements of a court opinion written by a student as a study guide and aid.

BURDEN OF PROOF. Although possessing several technical meanings, it generally refers to the duty of one of the parties to a suit to demonstrate that the weight of evidence or law is on his or her side. Sometimes the burden of proof will shift. In Anglo-American criminal justice the burden of proof is upon the prosecution.

CALENDAR. A list of cases in the order in which they are to be heard during a court term. Sometimes known as a court docket or trial list.

CANON LAW. The well-developed body of laws governing ecclesiastical matters of a Christian church; usually thought of in relationship to the Roman Catholic Church.

CAPITATION TAX. A head tax. A tax on persons regardless of such matters as income, assets, status, personal wealth.

CASE AND CONTROVERSY. Legal dispute with bona fide adversaries involving live and real issues. Not hypothetical or abstract issues, rights, or claims to be protected.

CASEBOOK. A law textbook containing leading edited judicial opinions on a particular legal subject. Cases are usually arranged chronologically by subject matter. First casebook published in 1871 authored by the Dean of the Harvard Law School: Langdell, *Selection of Cases on the Law Contracts.*

CASE LAW. The law as handed down in written judicial opinions.

CASE METHOD. A rigorous and dominant approach to legal education stressing the reading and in-depth analysis of leading judicial opinions. The growth of the law is traced through the reading of the cases. Professors employ the Socratic questioning method in connection with the cases. Critics of the case method contend that it produces socially myopic attorneys.

CAUSE OF ACTION. The existence of sufficient facts to warrant a law suit brought by a plaintiff.

CAVEAT EMPTOR. Latin for let the buyer beware. A warning to a buyer of a product that he purchases at his own risk.

CERTIFICATION. A method of appeal by which a lower court requests a higher court to answer certain questions of law so that the lower court may make a correct decision in light of the answer provided.

CERTIORARI, WRIT OF. An order from a superior to an inferior court to send the entire record of a case to the superior court for review. A discretionary writ employed by the U.S. Supreme Court.

CHAMBERS. The private office of a judge. Legal activity transacted there is often referred to as ''in chambers.''

CHANCERY, COURT OF. An old English court dealing with equity matters. In America most state governments have merged the chancery and law courts into one.

CHARTER. A document emanating from government granting certain rights, liberties, or powers to an organization, colony, local government, corporation, or people; *e.g.,* city charter, colonial charter, corporation charter, Magna Carta.

CHATTEL. Personal property excluding land.

CHIEF JUSTICE. The person appointed by the President with the advice and consent of the Senate to head the U.S. Supreme Court.

CIVIL ACTION. A lawsuit typically brought by a private party for the redress of a noncriminal act. Usually the plaintiff seeks money damages for the wrongful conduct of the defendant. For example, suits in negligence, contract, or defamation.

CIVIL LAW. (A) The system of jurisprudence based upon Roman law found in most Western European nation-states. It is distinct from the common law. (B) In common law countries, civil law refers to noncriminal legal matters.

CLASS ACTION SUIT. A legal suit brought by one person on behalf of himself and all others similarly situated. For example, John Doe, as representative of the class of all persons similarly situated, and for himself, Plaintiff, v. Paul Smith, in his capacity as Chief of Police of the City of XYZ, Defendant.

COMITY. The willingness to extend courtesy and respect to another nation-state or a unit of government within a state motivated by good will and a desire for good relations.

COMMON LAW. The system of law created by the English courts and brought to America by the colonists. Judges are said to find the law in the customs and habits of the people. It is largely judge-made law as distinct from statutory law made by legislators. Its chief competitor is the Roman-founded civil law system of Western Europe.

COMMUTATION OF PUNISHMENT. The reduction of a criminal penalty to a lesser punishment. Differs from a pardon in that it does not require the consent of the convict.

COMPLAINT. The plaintiff's initial pleading that frames the issues in the suit.

CONCURRENT JURISDICTION. The authority possessed by two or more courts to hear cases on a given subject.

CONCURRENT POWER. The political authority to exercise independent power by more than one government on the same subject matter. For example, the police and taxing powers in a federal system.

CONFEDERATION. An association or league among sovereign entities in which a central government is given certain limited responsibilities not affecting the basic powers of member entities or states.

CONFLICT OF LAWS. Refers to the field of law dealing with the situation in which a judge must choose among the laws of more than one jurisdiction as to which should apply in a particular case.

CONSPIRACY. Two or more persons acting together to accomplish a criminal objective or to pursue a noncriminal purpose in an unlawful or criminal manner.

CONSTITUTIONAL COURTS. A court named in a constitution or a court given certain protections independent of the other political branches of government. For the U.S. government, a constitutional court is one authorized under Article III of the Constitution or designated by the Congress as an Article III court. Article III courts are protected as to jurisdiction, appointments, and tenure.

CONSTITUTIONALISM. The principle of the rule of law under which the rulers abide by certain rules limiting their official conduct in return for the right to exercise authority.

CONTEMPT. An act that in some way obstructs or denigrates the dignity of a court, a legislative body, or an administrative agency. Usually a punishable offense.

COOPERATIVE FEDERALISM. A general approach to the American federal system that views the relationship between the national and state governments as a working partnership by which the mutual interests of both may be satisfied. Some take a more extreme view by stressing the "necessity" of national supremacy.

CORPUS DELICTI. Latin for the body of the crime. The production of evidence such as a dead body or a burned building indicating that the specific charge has in fact been committed and that some individual or group is criminally responsible.

CORPUS JURIS CIVILIS. The body of Roman law including the Digests, the Institutes, and the Novelae of Justinian. Latin for the body of civil law.

COUNT. Separate and independent claims or charges in a civil or criminal matter. A criminal indictment, for example, may contain many counts which if the prosecution should lose on one or more will still have others on which to convict.

COUNTERCLAIM. Constituting a separate cause of action, it is a claim made by the defendant against the plaintiff. Such a practice occurs in civil suits.

COURT OF LAST RESORT. A popular term referring to a court from which there is no appeal.

CRIME. A violation of government's penal laws. The offense is against society and not just a violation of another's individual rights.

CRIMINOLOGY. A social science concerned with the various causes, prevention, and punishment of crime. Considered a branch of sociology.

CULPABLE. A term referring to blame-worthy or wrongful conduct. Faultable.

CURIA. Latin for court.

DAMAGES. Money awarded by a court to a plaintiff for the wrongful conduct of the defendant.

DECLARATORY JUDGMENT. A judicial determination of the legal rights of the parties involved in an actual case or controversy, but where the court does not require the parties to abide by the judgment. Differs from an advisory opinion because there is an actual case or controversy.

DECREE. A court order or sentence specifying the details of a legal settlement, *e.g.*, terms of alimony or child custody. A consent decree is an agreement among the parties to conduct their affairs in a certain way. It cannot be amended without the consent of both parties.

DE FACTO. Refers to the existence of something in fact or in reality as distinguished from de jure, by right. For example, segregation in housing due to custom but not the result of official government action is often termed de facto segregation.

DEFAMATION. The damage to another's reputation by a false statement. *See* Libel; Slander.

DEFENDANT. In a court case, the one against whom a civil or criminal charge is brought.

DE JURE. Refers to lawful, rightful, or legitimate; opposite of de facto. For example, segregation in public education mandated by state law was known as de jure segregation.

DELIBERATION. The process of weighing reasons or evidence for or against a course of action. Usually applies to the work of a jury when determining guilt or innocence.

DE MINIMUS NON CURAT LEX. Latin term meaning that the law is not concerned with trivialities.

DEMURRER. A legal procedure permitting counsel to object to the sufficiency of a legal cause of action contained in the pleadings of the other side. Even if the act complained of did in fact occur, the law as presented by the other side does not cover that situation.

DE NOVO. A Latin term for anew, once more, again. Usually applies to a case being retried upon order of an appellate court. Some court systems permit de novo appeals.

DEPOSITION. A legal process to take the sworn testimony of a witness out of court. Usually both plaintiff and defendant attorneys are present and participate.

DICTA. *See* Obiter dicta.

DIVERSITY JURISDICTION. Refers to the authority of federal courts to hear cases involving citizens of different states.

DOCKET. A listing of cases to be heard by a court.

DOUBLE JEOPARDY. Tried twice for the same crime. Prohibited by U.S. Consitution.

DUAL FEDERALISM. The general approach to the American federal system that views the relationship between the national and state governments as adversarial. Best represented by the states' rights position that views the powers of the central government as strictly limited by the enumerated provisions in the Constitution; all other powers are reserved to the states by way of the Tenth Amendment.

ECCLESIASTICAL COURTS. In England, those courts dealing with spiritual matters presided over by members of the clergy; not part of the judicial system of the United States.

EMINENT DOMAIN. The right and ability of government to take private property for a public use.

EN BANC. Sometimes appearing as *En Banke,* meaning all the judges of a court or all jury members sitting together to hear a case.

EQUITY. The administration of justice based upon principles of fairness rather than strictly applied rules found in the common law. Because the common law courts of England became too rigid, equity courts were created; in the U.S., courts of law and courts of equity have largely been merged.

ERROR, WRIT OF. A method of appeal by which an appellate court orders a lower court to send a case to the higher court for review of alleged mistakes (errors) made by the lower court. Matters of law and not of fact are reviewed. The U.S. Supreme Court no longer employs this appeal method.

ESCHEAT. If the rightful owner or heir of property cannot be located, the property goes to the state.

EXCLUSIVE JURISDICTION. The sole authority vested in one court to hear a case on a given subject-matter; *e.g.,* for the U.S. Supreme Court, suits between and among the states, foreign ambassadors, bankruptcy, prosecutions of federal criminal law.

EXCLUSIVE POWER. The sole exercise of authority by one governmental body; *e.g.,* the U.S. national government possesses sole authority to make war.

EXECUTIVE AGREEMENT. An international agreement made by the President under his constitutional authority as commander-in-chief and in his capacity as the nation's spokesperson in foreign affairs. These agreements do not require senatorial approval as is the case for a treaty.

EXECUTIVE ORDERS. A directive from the President requiring the implementation of policy. The source of this authority stems from congressional authorization with the President as chief executive spelling out the details of policy implementation.

EX PARTE. A judicial hearing when only one party is present, such as when the appellant is in prison.

EX POST FACTO LAW. Latin for a law after the fact. An ex post facto law attempts to make an act a crime that was not a crime when it was done. Specifically prohibited by the U.S. Constitution.

EX. REL. An abbreviation for *Ex Relatione* meaning upon relation or information. A designation appearing in case titles indicating that the suit is instituted by a state but at the instigation or insistence of an individual; *e.g., Missouri ex. rel. Gaines* v. *S.W. Canada.* The state of Missouri is bringing the suit at the instigation of Lloyd Gaines against S.W. Canada.

EXTRADITION. The surrender of a fugitive by one jurisdiction to another.

FEDERAL QUESTION DOCTRINE. Those cases which directly involve the U.S. Constitution, the laws of the U.S. or treaties of the U.S. The U.S. Supreme Court has often maintained that its jurisdiction is limited to federal questions; one method of exercising judicial self-restraint.

FEDERATION. A structure of government dividing powers between the central and state governments; both the state and national governments operate directly upon the people.

FELONY. A crime designated by statute as serious. More serious than a misdemeanor, it may involve capital punishment or imprisonment for a long duration.

FIDUCIARY. A relationship in which one person acts in a position of trust for another. Sometimes involves management of money or property.

GERRYMANDERING. The drawing of legislative or other political district boundaries in such a manner as to give an advantage to one political party or interest.

GRAND JURY. A jury of inquiry designed to determine whether there is sufficient evidence to justify a criminal trial.

HABEAS CORPUS, WRIT OF. A writ directing that a person held in custody be brought before the court to determine if he or she is being lawfully held.

HISTORICAL JURISPRUDENCE. The application of the method of historical criticism to the study of law. Historical jurists study the customs and historical development of a people and their law. In the U.S., the employment of the case method is its greatest manifestation. Lead by the writings of Karl Von Savigny, Sir Henry Maine, and Christopher Columbus Langdell.

HUNG JURY. A jury that cannot agree upon a verdict. May result in a new trial.

IGNORAMUS. From the Latin meaning we are ignorant or we ignore it. A formal designation employed by a grand jury when it finds insufficient evidence to warrant an indictment.

IMMUNITY. An exemption from performing a duty. The grant of immunity in a criminal prosecution exempts a person from prosecution on the condition that he or she provides desired information.

IN CAMERA. Latin for vaulted chamber. A device by which a judge hears a case or part of a case in his chambers with spectators excluded.

INDICTMENT. A written accusation presented by a grand jury to a court charging one or more individuals with having committed a public offense.

IN FORMA PAUPERIS. Latin term meaning in the manner of a pauper. It is a device for indigents to sue without liability for costs. Provided for by U.S. statutory law permitting any citizen upon the execution of an oath to enter proceedings in any federal court. The most celebrated case reaching the U.S. Supreme Court in this manner is *Gideon* v. *Wainwright*.

INFORMATION. A device replacing indictment by grand jury in which the prosecutor submits his charges supported by evidence and sworn testimony to a trial court. Employed in England and many jurisdictions in the U.S.

INJUNCTION. A court order directing someone to do something or refrain from doing something.

IN PERSONAM. Latin meaning toward a person or individual. It is a legal action taken against an individual and not against the whole world.

INQUISITORIAL SYSTEM. A criminal justice system which assumes implicitly the guilt of the defendant, as opposed to common law systems. Civil law systems are said to employ this procedure; however, this characterization is not entirely correct because the highly professional magistrates take great care in reaching truth.

IN RE. Latin referring to the matter of. Employed in entitling judicial proceedings where there are no adversary parties; *e.g., In re: Smith.*

IN REM. A legal action to enforce property rights against the whole world and not one brought to enforce a legal right against individuals (In personam).

INTEGRATED BAR. A system of bar organization requiring all practicing attorneys within a state to belong to one organization (bar association). The integrated bar plan came from Canada, and North Dakota was the first state to adopt it. A closed shop, in labor terms.

INTERNATIONAL LAW. The law governing relations among nation-states. It is a body of general principles and rules accepted by the international community as binding. Because there is no sovereign authority some do not consider international law as law properly so-called.

INTERSTATE COMPACT. An agreement between two or more states, ratified by law of each state and approved by Congress.

INTESTATE. Dying without a will.

IPSE DIXIT. Latin for he himself said it. An arbitrary statement depending on the authority of the one who said it.

IPSO FACTO. Latin for by the fact itself. The fact speaks for itself.

JUDICIAL REVIEW. The power of a court to examine legislative enactments and acts of executive officials to determine their validity with respect to a written constitution; *e.g.*, *Marbury* v. *Madison*.

JUDICIAL SELF-RESTRAINT. The position accepted by many that judges should refrain from substituting their values for those of political decision-makers closer to the sentiments of the people. Operationally, the U.S. Supreme Court has devised various techniques of restraint so as to defer to other decisionmakers.

JURISPRUDENCE. (A) The Philosophy or science of law. (B) Sometimes refers to a body of law.

JURY. A group of persons charged by a law court with the duty to examine facts and determine the truth.

JUS SANGUINIS. Latin for right of blood. Refers to gaining citizenship by virtue of being born of parents who are citizens.

JUS SOLI. Latin for the right of land. Refers to gaining citizenship by virtue of place or country in which a person is born.

JUSTICE OF THE PEACE. Usually an elected official in rural areas with jurisdiction over minor civil or criminal matters.

LARCENY. The theft of the personal property of another. Stealing.

LEGAL REALIST SCHOOL OF JURISPRUDENCE. A heterodox group of scholars sharing a cynical attitude toward the law. They are concerned with the actual as opposed to an idealized notion of the operation of law. Applies the social scientific approach to the study of law, lead by such giants as Karl Llewellyn and Jerome Frank.

LEGISLATIVE COURTS. Courts established by the legislature. For the U.S. government, legislative courts are not protected by Article III. *See* Constitutional courts.

LEGISLATIVE INTENT. Refers to the motives of legislators when enacting a law. Usually involves a reading and interpreting by a court of the legislative history of a statute.

LIABILITY. Responsibility for performing a legally enforceable duty or obligation resulting from the commission of a wrongful act.

LIBEL. The written expression of a falsehood about another resulting or tending to result in damage to reputation. The written form of defamation of character, the other being slander, or spoken defamation.

LIEN. The legal right to possess property of another as security against a debt. If the debt is not paid or discharged, the property may be sold to satisfy the debt obligation.

LITIGANT. An active participant in a lawsuit; *e.g., Smith* v. *Jones.* Both Smith and Jones are litigants.

MALPRACTICE. Refers to professional misconduct or the below-standard performance of professional skills. Usually applies to suits against physicians and lawyers.

MANDAMUS, WRIT OF. Latin for we command. It is a court order commanding a public official or government agency to perform a certain act. It may apply to all branches of government.

MANSLAUGHTER. The crime of taking the life of another without malice.

MARTIAL LAW. The displacement of civilian law and government by the military. Rules usually depend solely upon the commands of the military ruler in charge and often tend to be arbitrary. Often imposed in time of war, insurrection, or coup d'etat.

MAXIM. A certain precept or axiom of law applied to all cases covered by its usage.

MECHANICAL JURISPRUDENCE. The widespread belief, held by many judges but discounted by political scientists, that judges only discover the law; they do not make it.

MEMORANDUM DECISION. A court ruling giving only what has been decided and what should be done but without the reasons for the decision.

MENS REA. Latin referring to the mind or guilt of the defendant. A chief function of juries in criminal trials is to ascertain the criminal intent (mens rea) of defendants.

MINISTERIAL. The carrying out of orders without making policy choices. No exercise of judgment or discretion.

MISCELLANEOUS DOCKET. The listing of in forma pauperis cases to be heard by the U.S. Supreme Court.

MISDEMEANOR. A criminal offense designated by statute to be of a lesser nature than a felony. Penalties are relatively minor.

MOOT. A discussion or argument of a hypothetical situation.

MOOT QUESTION. In a lawsuit, when the situation changes so that the relief sought is no longer applicable. For example, if during the course of a lengthy lawsuit for admission to a professional school, the student petitioner in fact graduates from the school then the question of admission becomes moot.

MOTION. A request by an attorney to the judge to take some action; *e.g.,* dismiss the case.

NATURAL LAW. A higher law transcending positive law; coming from God, nature, the universe, or reason; it lacks the ability to enforce commands.

NATURAL LAW SCHOOL OF JURISPRUDENCE. A school of law that posits the existence of universal principles of justice. It is concerned with what the law ought to be and thus is an ideal perspective for criticizing what the law is. Although ancient in origin, this school is enjoying renewed interest.

NEGLIGENCE. A subfield of tort law dealing with cases in which it is alleged that the defendant failed to exercise reasonable care, thereby resulting in injury or harm to another, some object, or thing.

NISI PRIUS. Latin meaning if not, unless before. Usually employed when referring to jury trial before a single judge as distinguished from an appellate court.

NOLO CONTENDERE. A Latin term meaning no contest. Without directly admitting guilt, it is a plea in a criminal proceeding in which the defendant does not offer a defense. A sentence is then handed down with the assumption of guilt.

NOVUS HOMO. Latin meaning a new man. Applied in reference to a person pardoned of a crime.

OBITER DICTA. That part of the reasoning of a judicial opinion which is not necessary or pertinent to the result reached by the court. It is extra and unnecessary verbiage included for a variety of reasons. Often simply referred to as dicta or obiter.

ORDINANCE. Usually refers to a local law.

PER CURIAM OPINION. A judicial opinion by the whole court expressing the views of the justices collectively.

PETITIONER. The party to a lawsuit who brings the case to a court by way of a petition; *e.g.*, the petition for a writ of certiorari. The party the petition is brought against is called the respondent.

PETIT JURY. A trial jury.

PLAIN MEANING RULE. When the language of a statute is clear and may be interpreted in only one way, a court employing this rule considers only the language and not other sources for assigning meaning to a statute.

PLAINTIFF. The party to a conflict who brings a lawsuit against another (defendant).

PLEA. The first pleading made by a defendant; a formal response to a criminal charge, for example, guilty, not guilty, or nolo contendere.

PLEA BARGAIN. The result of negotiation and compromise between the prosecution and defense by which the prosecution agrees to reduce the charges or counts in return for the defendant's guilty plea. The defendant, in these cases, is said to "cop a plea."

PLEADINGS. The formal and technical written statements made by the litigants framing the issues brought before a court.

POLITICAL QUESTION DOCTRINE. A principle of judicial self-restraint holding that certain issues are best left to the other coordinate branches of government; such issues are said to be nonjusticiable.

POSITIVE LAW. Man-made law enacted by a ruler, judge, or a legislature of some kind.

PRECEDENT. A previously decided judicial opinion which serves as a guide for the decision in a present case. The facts of the past and present cases must be deemed sufficiently similar to serve as a precedent.

PRESENTMENT. A device by which a grand jury acting on its own, without the consent or participation of a public prosecutor, formally accuses persons of criminal offenses. It differs from an indictment because the grand jury acts without the prosecutor.

PRIMA FACIE. Latin for at first sight, on first view. Prima facie evidence is such evidence that, if not later contradicted or in some way explained, is sufficient to sustain one's claim. A prima facie case is one that has proceeded to the point where it will support the charge if not later contradicted.

PRIVATE LAW. (A) A statute enacted dealing with one person or a group. For example, a law passed to compensate Mr. Smith for damage to his property because of Army exercises. (B) A generic term referring to the law governing conflicts among private parties; *e.g.,* contracts, property, torts, divorce.

PROCEDURAL LAW. The various and often complex rules governing the conduct of court cases.

PROPERTY. Ownership divided into two major parts. Real property, ownership in land, and personal property, ownership in movable objects or chattels.

PUBLIC LAW. (A) A statute enacted dealing with the society as a whole; *e.g.,* minimum wage laws, energy legislation, reorganization of governmental agencies. In Congress, such laws are given a number, *e.g.,* "Public Law No. 35." (B) A generic term referring to laws governing operations of government and the government's relationships with persons; *e.g.,* constitutional law, criminal law, administrative law.

PUNITIVE DAMAGES. Sometimes called "exemplary damages," it is awarded for malicious or willful harm inflicted by the defendant in a civil case. It is money damages awarded by a court over and beyond actual and compensatory damages for the harm suffered. It is intended to act as a warning and deterrent against future wrongful conduct.

QUAERE. A question or query involving a matter in doubt.

QUID PRO QUO. That which is given in return for something else, something for something. In contract law it constitutes legal consideration.

QUORUM. The number of members in an organization or body required to conduct business. Often a quorum is set at a majority of the entire membership.

RATIO DECIDENDI. Latin for the ground or reason for the decision. The very essence or central core of a judicial opinion, the principle of the case. To find the ratio decidendi the reader must establish which facts are treated by the judge as material and immaterial and his or her decision based upon them.

REAL PROPERTY. Ownership of land.

RECUSATION. Because of possible prejudice, a judge is disqualified from hearing a case. May be requested through motion of litigants or may be voluntary.

REMEDY. The legal means through a court order to enforce a right or to redress or compensate for a harm.

RES JUDICATA. Sometimes res a judicata. Latin for a thing decided. It is a fundamental principle in civil proceedings that once a conflict has been decided by the court the decision is conclusive and the parties may not bring the same case before the court again.

RES NOVA. Latin for a new thing or matter. Refers to a new legal question which has not been decided before.

RESPONDENT. The party to a lawsuit against whom a petition is brought. Also called an appellee.

RESTITUTION. To restore or to make good on something. For example, to return or pay for a stolen item.

RIGHT. The legal ability to perform or refrain from the performance of actions or the ability to control objects in one's possession. It also entails the ability to control the actions of others. In a legal sense, a right is enforceable at law as distinguished from a moral right.

SCIENTER. With knowledge; prior knowledge that the act was wrong.

SCINTILLA. A particle, the least bit. Usually refers to the least particle of evidence in a case.

SELF-EXECUTING. Legislative enactments, judicial decisions, agreements, or documents requiring no further official action to be implemented.

SEQUESTER. To isolate. For example, when during a trial the jury is kept from having contacts with the outside world.

SERIATIM. From the Latin meaning individually, one by one, in order, point by point. The practice of each judge writing and recording his own views of a case. This practice is opposed to a collective opinion of the court representing the views of the majority, minority, or the whole court. Before the accession of John Marshall to the U.S. Supreme Court, the seriatim practice was generally employed.

SHOW CAUSE ORDER. A command to a person to appear in court to explain why the court should not take a proposed course of action or accept a point of law before it.

SLANDER. The oral expression of a falsehood about another resulting or tending to result in damage to reputation. One form of defamation of character, the other being libel.

SOCIOLOGICAL JURISPRUDENCE. A school of jurisprudence that attempts to make the study of law a social science by substituting social psychological conceptions for legal notions such as the origins of law and the impact of law upon human society. It is also prescriptive. Roscoe Pound is generally viewed as the intellectual father of this school.

SOLICITORS. One segment of the legal profession in England. They do the routine office work dealing with clients directly and prepare cases for the barristers who argue in the higher courts.

STANDING TO SUE. Sometimes referred to as simply, standing. The necessity of a plaintiff to demonstrate that he or she has a personal and vital interest in the outcome of the legal case or controversy brought before the court.

STARE DECISIS. Latin for let the decision stand, abide by or adhere to decided cases. A deeply-rooted common law tradition that once a court has determined a legal principle for a given set of facts, all future cases with similar facts should be decided in the same way.

STATUTE. A law enacted by a legislative body.

STATUTE OF LIMITATIONS. A legislative enactment prescribing a limited time period within which a legal suit my be started for a given offense.

SUBPOENA. An order by a court or other duly authorized body to appear and testify before it.

SUBPOENA DUCES TECUM. An order directed toward a person by a court or other duly authorized body to appear before it with certain papers, documents, or other things.

SUBSTANTIVE LAW. The basic law governing relationships; *e.g.,* criminal law, constitutional law, property law, family law, torts. Substantive law is to be contrasted with procedural law; *e.g.,* law of evidence.

SUFFRAGE. The right to vote.

SUMMARY PROCEEDING. Any judicial business conducted before a court which is disposed of in a quick and simplified manner. Sometimes without a jury or indictment. For the U.S. Supreme Court it entails a judgment without the benefit of hearing oral arguments.

SUMMONS. A legal notice to a named defendant that he or she is being sued and must appear in court at a given time and place.

TEST CASE. A lawsuit brought to clarify, overturn, or establish a legal principle. Usually sponsored by an interest group, but nevertheless there is a bona fide litigant.

TORT. A civil wrong or injury inflicted upon another. It does not include contract matters. Examples include negligence, defamation of character, and wrongful death.

TRANSCRIPT OF RECORD. It is a printed copy (sometimes typed) of the proceedings of a court case. It is used by an appellate court in reviewing the proceedings below.

TREATY. A formal agreement between or among sovereign states creating rights and obligations under international law. In the U.S. all treaties must be ratified by two-thirds vote of the Senate.

TRIAL DE NOVO. *See* De novo.

ULTRA VIRES. Latin meaning outside or beyond authority or power. A term indicating an action taken outside the legal authority of the person or body performing it.

VENUE. The location within a jurisdiction where a legal dispute is tried by a court.

VOIR DIRE EXAMINATION. Examination, by legal counsel and the judge, of a potential jury member as to his or her competency to serve.

WAIVER. The relinquishing or giving up of a legally enforceable right, privilege, or benefit with full knowledge and voluntarily. For example, when a criminal defendant gives up his right to remain silent by taking the witness stand on his own behalf.

WARRANT. A legal instrument issued by a judicial magistrate to arrest someone or to search premises.

WRIT. An order in the form of a letter from a court commanding that something be done.

WRIT OF CERTIORARI. *See* Certiorari, Writ of.

WRIT OF ERROR. *See* Error, Writ of.

WRIT OF MANDAMUS. *See* Mandamus, Writ of.

6

Selected Bibliography

THE JUDICIAL SYSTEM

Abraham, Henry J. *The Judicial Process*. 4th ed. New York: Oxford University Press, 1980.

Ball, Howard. *Courts and Politics: The Federal Judicial System*. Englewood Cliffs, N.J.: Prentice-Hall, 1980.

Baum, Lawrence. *The Supreme Court*. Washington, D.C.: Congressional Quarterly Press, 1981.

Choper, Jesse H. *Judicial Review and the National Political Process: A Functional Reconsideration of the Role of the Supreme Court*. Chicago: University of Chicago Press, 1980.

Congressional Quarterly. *Guide to the U.S. Supreme Court*. Washington, D.C.: Congressional Quarterly, Inc., 1979.

Ducat, Craig R. *Modes of Constitutional Interpretation*. St. Paul, Mn.: West Publishing Co., 1978.

Ely, John Hart. *Democracy and Distrust: A Theory of Judicial Review*. Cambridge: Harvard University Press, 1980.

Gabin, Sanford Byron. *Judicial Review and the Reasonable Doubt Test*. Port Washington, N.Y.: Kennikat Press, 1980.

Goldman, Sheldon, and Jahnige, Thomas P. *The Federal Courts as a Political System*. 2d ed. New York: Harper & Row, 1976.

Goldman, Sheldon and Sarat, Austin. *American Court Systems: Readings in Judicial Process and Behavior*. San Francisco: W.H. Freeman, 1978.

Horowitz, Donald L. *The Courts and Social Policy*. Washington, D.C.: Brookings Institution, 1977.

Jackson, Robert H. *The Supreme Court in the American System of Government*. Cambridge: Harvard University Press, 1955.

Jacob, Herbert. *Justice in America: Courts, Lawyers, and the Judical Process*. 3rd ed. Boston: Little, Brown, 1978.

McLauchlan, William P. *American Legal Processes*. New York: John Wiley & Sons, 1977.

Murphy, Walter F., and Pritchett, C. Herman. *Courts, Judges, and Politics*. 3rd ed. New York: Random House, 1979.

Neubauer, David W. *America's Courts and the Criminal Justice System*. North Scituate, Ma.: Duxbury Press, 1979.

Oakley, John Bilyeu, and Thompson, Robert S. *Law Clerks and the Judicial Process: Perceptions of the Qualities and Functions of Law Clerks in American Courts.* Bekeley: University of California Press, 1980.

Peltason, Jack W. *Federal Courts in the Political Process.* New York: Random House, 1955.

Provine, Doris Marie. *Case Selection in the United States Supreme Court.* Chicago: University of Chicago Press, 1980.

Radcliffe, James E. *The Case or Controversy Provision.* University Park: Pennsylvania State University Press, 1978.

Rohde, David W., and Spaeth, Harold J. *Supreme Court Decision Making.* San Francisco: Freeman, 1976.

Schmidhauser, John R. *Judges and Justices: The Federal Appellate Judiciary.* Boston: Little, Brown, 1979.

Spaeth, Harold J. *Supreme Court Policy Making: Explanation and Prediction.* San Francisco: W.H. Freeman, 1979.

Stern, Robert L., and Gressman, Eugene. *Supreme Court Practice.* 5th ed. Washington, D.C.: The Bureau of National Affairs, Inc., 1978.

Ulmer, S. Sidney, ed. *Courts, Law, and Judicial Processes.* New York: The Free Press, 1981.

Wasby, Stephen L. *The Supreme Court in the Federal Judicial System.* New York: Holt, Rinehart and Winston, 1978.

Woodward, Bob, and Armstrong, Scott. *The Brethren: Inside the Supreme Court.* New York: Simon & Schuster, 1979.

JURISPRUDENCE

Ackerman, Bruce A. *Social Justice in the Liberal State.* New Haven: Yale University Press, 1980.

Austin, John. *Lectures on Jurisprudence.* 2 vols. New York: James Crockcraft, 1875.

Bishin, William R., and Stone, Christopher D. *Law, Language, and Ethics: An Introduction to Law and Legal Method.* Mineola, New York: The Foundation Press, Inc. 1972.

Bodenheimer, Edgar. *Jurisprudence: The Philosophy and Method of the Law.* Rev. ed. Cambridge: Harvard University Press, 1974.

Brkić, Jovan. *Norm and Order: An Investigation into Logic, Semantics, and the Theory of Law and Morals.* New York: Humanities Press, 1970.

Cardozo, Benjamin. *The Nature of the Judicial Process.* New Haven: Yale University Press, 1921.

Carter, Lief H. *Reason in Law.* Boston: Little, Brown, 1979.

Cohen, Morris. *Reason and Law.* New York: The Free Press, 1950.

d'Entreves, A. P. *Natural Law: An Introduction to Legal Philosophy.* 2nd ed. London: Hutchinson, 1970/77.

Frank, Jerome. *Courts on Trial: Myth and Reality in American Justice.* Princeton: Princeton University Press, 1949.

Friedrich, Carl Joachim. *The Philosophy of Law in Historical Perspectives.* 2nd ed. Chicago: University of Chicago Press, 1963.

Fuller, Lon. *The Morality of Law.* New Haven: Yale University Press, 1964.

Hall, Jerome. *Foundations of Jurisprudence*. Indianapolis: Bobbs-Merrill, 1973.

————. *Readings in Jurisprudence*. Indianapolis: Bobbs-Merrill, 1938.

Hart. H.L.A. *The Concept of Law*. Oxford: Clarendon, 1961.

Levi, Edward. *An Introduction to Legal Reasoning*. Chicago: University of Chicago Press, 1949.

Llewellyn, Karl. *The Bramble Bush*. New York: Oceana Publications, 1930.

————. *The Common Law Tradition: Deciding Appeals*. Boston: Little, Brown, 1962.

Morris, Clarence, ed. *The Great Legal Philosophers: Selected Readings in Jurisprudence*. Philadelphia: University of Pennsylvania Press, 1971.

Patterson, Edwin W. *Jurisprudence: Men and Ideas of the Law*. Brooklyn: The Foundation Press, 1953.

Pound, Roscoe. *An Introduction to the Philosophy of Law*. Rev. ed. New Haven: Yale University Press, 1954.

Rawls, John. *A Theory of Justice*. Cambridge: Belknap Press of Harvard University Press, 1971.

Savigny, Friedrick K. *Of the Vocation of Our Age for Legislation and Jurisprudence*. Translated by A. Hayward. London: Littlewood, 1831.

Shklar, Judith N. *Legalism*. Cambridge: Harvard University Press, 1964.

Zelermyer, William. *The Process of Legal Reasoning*. Englewood Cliffs: Prentice-Hall, 1963.

CONSTITUTION LAW—GENERAL

Congressional Quarterly. *The Supreme Court: Justice and the Law*. 2d ed. Washington, D.C.: Congressional Quarterly, 1977.

Congressional Research Service, Library of Congress. *The Constitution of the United States of America: Analysis and Interpretation*. Washington: U.S. Government Printing Office, 1973.

Corwin, Edward S. *The Constitution and What It Means Today*. 14th ed. Revised by Harold W. Chase and Craig R. Ducat. Princeton: Princeton University Press, 1978.

Peltason, J.W. *Understanding the Constitution*. 8th ed. New York: Holt, Rinehart and Winston, 1979.

Pritchett, C. Herman. *The American Constitution*. 3rd ed. New York: McGraw-Hill, 1977.

————. *The American Constitutional System*. 5th ed. New York: McGraw-Hill, 1981.

Schwartz, Bernard. *Constitutional Law: A Textbook*. 2d ed. New York: Macmillan, 1979.

Tribe, Laurence H. *American Constitutional Law*. Mineola, N.Y.: The Foundation Press, 1978.

Williams, Jerre S. *Constitutional Analysis in a Nutshell*. St. Paul, Minn.: West, 1979.

CONSTITUTIONAL HISTORY

Adams, Willi Paul. *The First American Constitutions: Republican Ideology and the Making of the State Constitutions in the Revolutionary Era*. Translated by Rita and Robert Kimberg. Chapel-Hill: University of North Carolina Press, 1980.

Amlund, Curtis Arthur. *Federalism in the Southern Confederacy.* Washington: Public Affairs Press, 1966.

Beard, Charles Austin. *An Economic Interpretation of the Constitution of the United States.* New York: Free Press, 1965.

_____. *The Federalist.* New York: F. Ungar, 1959.

_____. *The Supreme Court and the Constitution.* Englewood Cliffs: Prentice-Hall, 1962.

Beth, Loren P. *The Development of the American Constitution, 1877–1917.* New York: Harper & Row, 1971.

Boorstin, Daniel J. *The Americans: The Colonial Experience.* New York: Random House, 1958.

Boyd, Steven R. *The Politics of Opposition: Antifederalists and the Acceptance of the Constitution.* Millwood, N.Y.: KTO Press, 1979.

Burgess, John William. *Recent Changes in American Constitutional Theory.* New York: Arno Press, 1972.

Burns, Edward McNall. *James Madison: Philosopher of the Constitution.* New York: Octagon Books, 1968.

Cope, Alfred Haines. *Franklin D. Roosevelt and the Supreme Court.* Lexington, Mass.: Heath, 1969.

Corwin, Edward S. *The Doctrine of Judicial Review.* Princeton: Princeton University Press, 1914.

Cox, Archibald. *The Warren Court.* Cambridge: Harvard University Press, 1968.

Crosskey, William W. *Politics and the Constitution in the History of the United States.* 2 vols. Chicago: University of Chicago Press, 1953.

Dewey, Donald O. *Marshall Versus Jefferson: The Political Background of Marbury v. Madison.* New York: Knopf, 1970.

_____. *Union and Liberty: A Documentary History of American Constitutionalism.* New York: McGraw-Hill, 1969.

Donovan, Frank Robert. *Mr. Madison's Constitution: the Story Behind the Constitutional Convention.* New York: Dodd, Mead, 1965.

Douglas, William O. *The Court Years, 1935–1975.* New York: Random House, 1980.

Dunning, William Archibald. *Essays on the Civil War and Reconstruction.* New York: Harper & Row, 1965.

Elliot, Jonathan. *The Debates in the Several State Conventions on the Adoption of the Federal Constitution as Recommended by the General Convention at Philadelphia in 1787.* New York: B. Franklin, 1968.

Farrand, Max. *The Framing of the Constitution of the United States.* New Haven: Yale University Press, 1913.

Farrand, Max, ed. *The Records of the Federal Convention of 1787.* 4 vols. New Haven: Yale University Press, 1937/1966.

Ford, Saul Leicester, ed. *The Federalist.* New York: H. Holt, 1898.

Funston, Richard Y. *Constitutional Counterrevolution? The Warren and the Burger Courts: Judicial Policy Making in Modern America.* New York: Halsted Press, 1977.

Green, Fletcher M. *Constitutional Development in the South Atlantic States.* New York: W. W. Norton, 1966.

Haines, Charles G. *The American Doctrine of Judicial Supremacy.* 2d ed. Berkeley: University of California Press, 1959.

_____. *The Role of the Supreme Court in American Government and Politics, 1789–1835.* Berkeley: University of California Press, 1944.

Haines, Charles G. and Sherwood, Foster H. *The Role of the Supreme Court in American Government and Politics, 1835–1864.* Berkeley: University of California Press, 1957.

Harmon, M. Judd, ed. *Essays on the Constitution of the United States.* Port Washington, N.Y.: Kennikat Press, 1978.

Hentoff, Nat. *The First Freedom: The Tumultuous History of Free Speech in America.* New York: Delacorte Press, 1980.

Higginbotham, A. Leon, Jr. *In the Matter of Color: Race and the American Legal Process, The Colonial Period.* New York: Oxford University Press, 1978.

Hirsch, H. N. *The Enigma of Felix Frankfurter.* New York: Basic Books, 1981.

Hockett, Homer Carey. *The Constitutional History of the United States.* New York: Macmillan, 1939.

Horwitz, Morton J. *The Transformation of American Law, 1780–1860.* Cambridge: Harvard University Press, 1977.

Howard, A. *The Road From Runnymede: Magna Carta and Constitutionalism in America.* Charlottesville: University of Virginia Press, 1968.

Hurst, Willard. *The Growth of American Law, The Law Makers.* Boston: Little, Brown, 1950.

Hyman, Harold Melvin. *A More Perfect Union: The Impact of the Civil War and Reconstruction on the Constitution.* Boston: Houghton Mifflin, 1975.

Kelly, Alfred Hinsey and Harbison, Winifred A. *The American Constitution: its Origins and Development.* 5th ed. New York: W. W. Norton, 1976.

Kenyon, Cecelia M. *The Antifederalists.* Indianapolis: Bobbs-Merrill, 1966.

Kurland, Philip B. *Politics, The Constitution, and the Warren Court.* Chicago: University of Chicago Press, 1970.

_____. *Supreme Court Review.* Chicago: University of Chicago Press. Annual since 1960.

Lash, Joseph P., ed. *From the Diaries of Felix Frankfurter.* New York: W. W. Norton, 1975.

Levy, Leonard Williams. *Essays on the Making of the Constitution.* New York: Oxford University Press, 1969.

Magee, James J. *Mr. Justice Black: Absolutist on the Court.* Charlottesville: University of Virginia Press, 1980.

Main, Jackson Turner. *The Antifederalists: Critics of the Constitution.* New York: W. W. Norton, 1974.

Marks, Frederick W. *Independence on Trial: Foreign Affairs and the Making of the Constitution.* Baton Rouge: Louisiana State University Press, 1973.

Mason, Alpheus Thomas. *The States Rights Debate: Antifederalism and the Constitution.* 2nd ed. New York: Oxford University Press, 1972.

_____. *The Supreme Court from Taft to Burger.* 3d ed. Baton Rouge: Louisiana State University Press, 1979.

_____. *The Supreme Court from Taft to Warren.* Baton Rouge: Louisiana State University Press, 1958.

McCloskey, Robert G. *The American Supreme Court.* Chicago: University of Chicago Press, 1960.

_____. *The Modern Supreme Court.* Martin Shapiro, ed. Cambridge: Harvard University Press, 1972.

McLaughlin, Andrew Cunningham, *The Confederation and the Constitution*. New York: Collier Books, 1971.

_____. *A Constitutional History of the United States*. New York: Appleton-Century-Crofts, 1963.

_____. *The Courts, the Constitution, and Parties: Studies in Constitutional History and Politics*. New York: Da Capo Press, 1972.

_____. *The Foundations of American Constitutionalism*. Gloucester, Mass.: P. Smith, 1972.

Millett, Stephen M. *A Selected Bibliography of American Constitutional History*. Santa Barbara, Cal.: Clio Books, 1975.

Mitchell, Broadus. *A Biography of the Constitution of the United States: Its Origin, Formation, Adoption, Interpretation*. 2d ed. New York: Oxford University Press, 1975.

Murphy, Paul L. *The Constitution in Crisis Times, 1918–1969*. New York: Harper & Row, 1972.

_____. *World War I and the Origin of Civil Liberties in the United States*. New York: W. W. Norton, 1979.

Nieman, Donald G. *To Set the Law in Motion: The Freedmen's Bureau and the Legal Rights of Blacks, 1865–1868*. Millwood, N.Y.: KTO Press, 1979.

Paludan, Phillip S. *A Covenant with Death: The Constitution, Law and Equality in the Civil War Era*. Urbana: University of Illinois Press, 1975.

Pfeffer, Leo. *This Honorable Court: A History of the Supreme Court of the United States*. Boston: Beacon Press, 1965.

Pollack, Louis. *The Constitution and the Superme Court: A Documentary History*. 2 vols. Cleveland: World Publishing Co., 1966.

Pritchett, C. Herman. *Civil Liberties and the Vinson Court*. Chicago: University of Chicago Press, 1954.

_____. *The Roosevelt Court: A Study of Judicial Votes and Values, 1937–1947*. New York: Macmillan, 1948.

Rodell, Fred. *Nine Men: A Political History of the Supreme Court from 1790–1955*. New York: Random House, 1955.

Rossiter, Clinton. *1787: The Grand Convention*. New York: Macmillan, 1966.

Rutland, Robert A. *The Birth of the Bill of Rights, 1776–1791*. New York: Macmillan, 1962.

Schwartz, Bernard. *From Confederation to Nation: The American Constitution, 1835–1877*. Baltimore: Johns Hopkins University Press, 1973.

Simon, James F. *Independent Journey: The Life of William O. Douglas*. New York: Harper and Row, 1980.

_____. *In His Own Image: The Supreme Court in Richard Nixon's America*. New York: David McKay, 1973.

Smith, David G. *The Convention and the Constitution: The Political Ideas of the Founding Fathers*. New York: St. Martin's Press, 1965.

Solberg, Winston U., ed. *The Federal Convention and the Formation of the Union of the American States*. Indianapolis: Bobbs-Merrill, 1958.

Steamer, Robert J. *The Supreme Court in Crisis: A History of Conflict*. Amherst: University of Massachusetts Press, 1971.

Sutherland, Arthur E. *Constitutionalism in America: Origin and Evolution of its Fundamental Ideas*. New York: Blaisdell Publishing, 1965.

Swisher, Carl Brent. *American Constitutional Development.* Boston: Houghton Mifflin, 1954.

_____. *The Growth of Constitutional Power in the United States.* Chicago: University of Chicago Press, 1963.

U.S. Congress. The Debates and Proceedings in the Congress of the United States. *A Second Federalist: Congress Creates a Government.* New York: Appleton-Century-Crofts, 1967.

U.S. Constitutional Convention, 1787. *Notes of Debates in the Federal Convention of 1787, reported by James Madison.* Athens: Ohio University Press, 1966.

U.S. Constitution. *The Constitution of the United States of America, with a Summary of the Actions by the States in Ratification of the Provisions thereof.* Richmond: Virginia Commission on Constitutional Government, 1965.

U.S. Constitution Sesquicentennial Commission. *History of the Formation of the Union Under the Constitution with Liberty Documents and Report of the Commission.* New York: Greenwood Press, 1968.

Vose, Clement E. *Constitutional Change: Amendment Politics and Supreme Court Litigation Since 1900.* Lexington, Mass.: Lexington Books, 1972.

Warren, Charles. *Congress, the Constitution and the Supreme Court.* New York: Johnson Reprint Corp., 1968.

_____. *The Making of the Constitution.* New York: Barnes & Noble, 1967.

_____. *The Supreme Court in United States History.* Boston: Little, Brown, 1947.

Wasby, Stephen L. *Continuity and Change: From the Warren Court to the Burger Court.* Pacific Palisades, Calif.: Goodyear Publishing, 1976.

Westin, Alan F. *An Autobiography of the Supreme Court.* New York: Macmillan, 1963.

Wood, S.B. *Constitutional Politics in the Progressive Era.* Chicago: University of Chicago Press, 1968.

Woodward, C. Vann. *The Strange Career of Jim Crow.* 3rd ed. New York, Oxford University Press, 1974.

Wright, Benjamin Fletcher. *The Growth of American Constitutional Law.* Chicago: University of Chicago Press, 1967.

FEDERALISM

Ackerman, B.A. *Private Property and the Constitution.* New Haven: Yale University Press, 1977.

Baxter, Maurice G. *The Steamboat Monopoly: Gibbons v. Ogden, 1824.* New York: Knopf, 1972.

Benson, Paul R., Jr. *The Supreme Court and the Commerce Clause.* New York: Dunellen, 1970.

Cooley, Thomas M. *Constitutional Limitations.* New York: Da Capo Press, 1972.

Cortner, Richard C. *The Jones and Laughlin Case.* New York: Knopf, 1970.

Corwin, Edward Samuel. *The Commerce Power Versus States Rights.* Magnolia, Mass.: Peter Smith, 1962.

Davis, S. Rufus. *The Federal Principle.* Berkeley: University of California Press, 1978.

Elazar, Daniel J. *American Federalism: A View From the States.* 2d ed. New York: Harper and Row, 1972.

Engdahl, D. E. *Constitutional Power: Federal and State.* St. Paul: West Publishing, 1974.

Flack, Horace, *The Adoption of the Fourteenth Amendment.* Baltimore: Johns Hopkins Press, 1908.

Folgelson, R. M., and Susskind, L. E. *American Federalism.* New York: Arno Press, 1977.

Frankfurter, Felix. *The Commerce Clause Under Marshall, Taney and Waite.* Chicago: Quadrangle Books, 1964.

Glendening, Parris N., and Reeves, Mavis Mann. *Pragmatic Federalism.* Pacific Palisades, Calif.: Palisades Publishers, 1977.

Grodzins, Morton. *The American System.* Chicago: Rand McNally, 1966.

Hallman, Howard W. *Emergency Employment: A Study of Federalism.* University, Ala.: University of Alabama Press, 1977.

Kenyon, Cecelia M., ed. *The Antifederalists.* New York: Bobbs Merrill, 1964.

Leach, Richard. *American Federalism.* New York: Oxford University Press, 1972.

Lewis, Frederick P. *The Dilemma in the Congressional Power to Enforce the Fourteenth Amendment.* Washington: University Press of America, 1980.

Magrath, C. Peter. *Yazoo: The Case of Fletcher v. Peck.* New York: W. W. Norton, 1966.

Mason, Alpheus Thomas. *The States Rights Debate: Antifederalism and the Constitution.* New York: Oxford University Press, 1972.

Reagan, Michael D. with John Sanzone. *The New Federalism.* 2d ed. New York: Oxford University Press, 1980.

Ridgeway, Marian E. *Interstate Compacts: A Question of Federalism.* Carbondale: Southern Illinois University Press, 1971.

Riker, William. *Federalism: Origin, Operation, Significance.* Boston: Little, Brown, 1964.

Schmidhauser, John R. *The Supreme Court as Final Arbiter in Federal/State Relations, 1789–1957.* Westport: Greenwood Press, 1973.

Sprague, John D. *Voting Patterns of the United States Supreme Court: Cases in Federalism, 1889–1959.* Indianapolis: Bobbs-Merrill, 1968.

Sunquist. James L. *Making Federalism Work.* Washington: Brookings Institution, 1969.

Tarr, George Alan. *Judicial Impact and State Supreme Courts.* Lexington, Mass.: Lexington Books, 1977.

Wheare, K.C. *Federal Government,* 4th ed. New York: Oxford University Press, 1963.

Wildavsky, Aaron. *American Federalism in Perspective.* Boston: Little, Brown, 1967.

Wright, Benjamin Fletcher. *The Contract Clause of the Constitution.* Cambridge: Harvard University Press, 1938.

CONGRESS

Barber, S.A. *The Constitution and the Delegation of Congressional Power.* Chicago: University of Chicago Press, 1975.

Baxter, M.G. *Daniel Webster and the Supreme Court.* Amherst: University of Massachusetts Press, 1967.

Berger, Raoul. *Congress Versus the Supreme Court.* Cambridge, Mass.: Harvard University Press, 1969.

Breckenridge, A.C. *Congress Against the Court.* Lincoln: University of Nebraska Press, 1970.

Claude, Richard. *The Supreme Court and the Electoral Process.* Baltimore: Johns Hopkins Press, 1970.

Congressional Quarterly. *Guide to the Congress of the United States: Origins, History, and Procedure.* Washington: Congressional Quarterly Service, 1971.

_____. *Impeachment and the United States Congress.* Washington: Congressional Quarterly, 1974.

Cortner, Richard C. *The Jones and Laughlin Case.* New York: Knopf, 1970.

Elliott, Ward E. Y. *The Rise of Guardian Democracy: The Supreme Court's Role in Voting Rights Disputes, 1845–1969.* Cambridge, Mass.: Harvard University Press, 1974.

Field, O.P. *Effect of an Unconstitutional Statute.* New York: Da Capo Press, 1971.

Fisher, Louis. *President and Congress: Power and Policy.* New York: Free Press, 1972.

_____. *The Constitution Between Friends: Congress, the President, and the Law.* New York: St. Martin's Press, 1978.

Flynn, John J. *Federalism and State Antitrust Regulation.* Ann Arbor: University of Michigan Law School, 1964.

Frankfurter, Felix. *The Commerce Clause under Marshall, Taney, and Waite.* Chicago: Quadrangle Books, 1964.

Gallagher, Hugh Gregory. *Advise and Obstruct: The Role of United States Senate in Foreign Policy Decisions.* New York: Delacarte Press, 1969.

Goodman, Walter. *The Committee: the Extraordinary Career of the House Committee on Un-American Activities.* New York: Farrar, Straus and Giroux, 1968.

Hamilton, James. *The Power to Probe.* New York: Vintage Books, 1977.

Lee, R. Alton. *A History of Regulatory Taxation.* Lexington, Ky.: University Press of Kentucky, 1973.

Letwin, William. *Law and Economic Policy in America: the Evolution of the Sherman Antitrust Act.* Edinburgh: Edinburgh University Press, 1967.

Magrath, C. Peter. *Yazoo: The Case of Fletcher v. Peck.* New York: W. W. Norton, 1967.

Mansfield, Harvey C., Sr. *Congress Against the President.* New York: Praeger, 1975.

McGeary, M. Nelson. *The Development of Congressional Investigating Power.* New York: Octagon Books, 1966.

Mendelson, Wallace. *Capitalism, Democracy, and the Supreme Court.* New York: Appleton-Century-Crofts, 1960.

Miller, Arthur S. *The Supreme Court and American Capitalism.* New York: Free Press, 1968.

Morgan, Donald Grant. *Congress and the Constitution: A Study of Responsibility.* Cambridge: Belknap Press of Harvard University Press, 1966.

Murphy, Walter F. *Congress and the Court: A Case Study in the American Political Process.* Chicago: University of Chicago Press, 1964.

Pritchett, C. Herman. *Congress Versus the Supreme Court.* Minneapolis: University of Minnesota Press, 1961.

Roche, John P., and Levy, Leonard. *The Congress.* New York: Harcourt, 1964.

Rothman, David J. *Politics and Power: The United States Senate, 1869–1901.* New York: Atheneum, 1969.

Schmidhauser, John R., and Berg, Larry L. *The Supreme Court and Congress: Conflict and Interaction, 1945-1968.* New York: Free Press, 1972.

Warren, Charles. *Congress, the Constitution and the Supreme Court.* New York: Johnson Reprint Corp., 1968.

Weeks, K.M. *Adam Clayton Powell and the Supreme Court.* New York: Dunellen, 1971.

Wilson, Woodrow. *Congressional Government.* Introduction by Walter Lippmann. Cleveland: Meridian Books, 1885, 1967.

PRESIDENCY

Abraham, Henry. *Justices and Presidents: A Political History of Appointments to the Supreme Court.* New York: Oxford University Press, 1974.

American Civil Liberties Union. *Why President Richard Nixon Should Be Impeached.* Washington: Public Affairs Press, 1973.

Amlund, Curtis Arthur. *New Perspectives on the Presidency.* New York: Philosophical Library, 1969.

Anderson, Donald F. *William Howard Taft: A Conservative's Conception of the Presidency.* Ithaca, N.Y.: Cornell University Press, 1973.

Barber, James D. *The Presidential Character.* 2d ed. Englewood Cliffs, N.J.: Prentice-Hall, 1977.

Benedict, Michael Les. *The Impeachment and Trial of Andrew Johnson.* New York: W. W. Norton, 1973.

Berger, Raoul. *Executive Privilege: A Constitutional Myth.* Cambridge, Ma.: Harvard University Press, 1974.

_____. *Impeachment: The Constitutional Problems.* Cambridge, Ma.: Harvard University Press, 1974.

Bickel, Alexander M. *Reform and Continuity: The Electoral College, the Convention and the Party System.* New York: Harper and Row, 1971.

Blackman, John L., Jr. *Presidential Seizure and Labor Disputes.* Cambridge, Ma.: Harvard University Press, 1967.

Brant, Irving. *Impeachment: Trials and Errors.* New York: Knopf, 1972.

Breckenridge, Adam Carlyle. *The Executive Privilege: Presidential Control over Information.* Lincoln: University of Nebraska Press, 1974.

Burns, James M. *Presidential Government: The Crucible of Leadership.* Boston: Houghton Mifflin, 1973.

Chase, Harold W. *Federal Judges: The Appointing Process.* Minneapolis: University of Minnesota Press, 1972.

Cronin, Thomas E., ed. *The Presidential Advisory System.* New York: Harper & Row, 1969.

Corwin, Edward S. *The President: Office and Powers.* 4th ed. New York: New York University Press, 1957.

Donovan, Robert J. *Conflict and Crisis: The Presidency of Harry S. Truman, 1945-1948.* New York: W. W. Norton, 1977.

Edwards, George C. III. *Presidential Influence in Congress.* San Francisco: Freeman, 1980.

Feerick, John D. *From Failing Hands: The Story of Presidential Succession.* New York: Fordham University Press, 1965.

Fisher, Louis. *The Constitution Between Friends: Congress, The President, and The Law.* New York: St. Martin's Press, 1978.

———. *President and Congress: Power and Policy.* New York: Free Press, 1973.

———. *Presidential Spending Power.* Princeton: Princeton University Press, 1975.

Genovese, Michael A. *The Supreme Court, the Constitution, and Presidential Power.* Washington: University Press of America, 1980.

Haight, David and Johnston, L., eds. *The President: Roles and Powers.* Chicago: Rand McNally, 1965.

Hardin, Charles M. *Presidential Power and Accountability.* Chicago: University of Chicago Press, 1974.

Hart, James. *The Ordinance-Making Powers of the President of the United States.* New York: Da Capo Press, 1970.

Henkin, Louis. *Foreign Affairs and the Constitution.* New York: Foundation Press, 1972.

Hirschfield, Robert S. *The Power of the Presidency.* 2nd ed. Chicago: Aldine Publishing, 1973.

Jackson, Carlton. *Presidential Vetos, 1792–1945.* Athens: University of Georgia Press, 1967.

Javits, Jacob Koppell. *Who Makes War: The President Versus Congress.* New York: Morrow, 1973.

Johnstone, Robert M. *Jefferson and the Presidency: Leadership in the Young Republic.* Ithaca: Cornell University Press, 1978.

Kallenbach, Joseph E. *The American Chief Executive.* New York: Harper and Row, 1966.

Koenig, Louis W. *The Chief Executive.* New York: Harcourt, Brace and World, 1968.

Labovitz, John R. *Presidential Impeachment.* New Haven: Yale University Press, 1978.

Latham, Earl. *Kennedy and Presidential Power.* Lexington, Ma.: Heath, 1972.

Longley, Lawrence D., and Braun, Alan G. *The Politics of Electoral College Reform* 2nd ed. New Haven: Yale University Press, 1975.

Merry, Henry J. *Constitutional Function of Presidential-Administrative Separation.* Washington: University Press of America, 1978.

———. *Five-Branch Government: The Full Measure of Constitutional Checks and Balances.* Urbana: University of Illinois Press, 1980.

Miller, Arthur S. *Presidential Power in a Nutshell.* St. Paul: West Publishing, 1977.

Milton, George Fort. *The Use of Presidential Power, 1789–1943.* New York: Octagon Book,. 1965.

Navasky, Victor. *Kennedy Justice.* New York: Atheneum, 1971.

Neustadt, Richard E. *Presidential Power: The Politics of Leadership from FDR to Carter.* New York: John Wiley & Sons, 1980.

Orman, John M. *Presidential Secrecy and Deception: Beyond the Power to Persuade.* Westport, Conn.: Greenwood Press, 1980.

Polsby, Nelson W. *Congress and the Presidency.* 2nd ed. Englewood Cliffs: Prentice-Hall, 1971.

Pusey, Merlo J. *The Way We Go to War.* Boston: Houghton Mifflin, 1969.

Roche, John, and Levy, Leonard. *The Presidency.* New York: Harcourt, Brace and World, 1964.

Rossiter, Clinton. *The Supreme Court and the Commander-in-Chief.* Ithaca: Cornell University Press, 1976.

Schlesinger, Arthur M., Jr. *The Imperial Presidency.* Boston: Houghton Mifflin, 1973.

Scigliano, Robert. *The Supreme Court and the Presidency.* New York: The Free Press, 1972.

Silva, Ruth C. *Presidential Succession.* Westport, Conn.: Greenwood, 1968.

Smith, John Malcolm. *Powers of the President During Crises.* New York: Da Capo Press, 1972.

Tugwell, Rexford G., and Cronin, T. E. *The Presidency Reappraised.* 2nd ed. New York: Praeger, 1977.

Westin, Alan F. *The Anatomy of a Constitutional Law Case.* New York: Macmillan, 1958.

Young, Donald. *American Roulette: The History and Dilemma of the Vice-Presidency.* New York: Holt, Rinehart and Winston, 1965.

CIVIL RIGHTS AND LIBERTIES

Abernathy, Glenn. *The Right of Assembly and Association.* Columbia: South Carolina University Press, 1961.

Abraham, Henry J. *Freedom and the Court: Civil Rights and Liberties in the United States.* 3rd ed. New York: Oxford University Press, 1977.

Anastapolo, George. *The Constitutionalist: Notes on the First Amendment.* Dallas: Southern Methodist University Press, 1971.

Baker, Gordon E. *The Reapportionment Revolution.* New York: Random House, 1966.

Barsh, Lawrence, and Henderson, James Youngblood. *The Road: Indian Tribes and Political Liberty.* Berkeley: University of California Press, 1980.

Becker, Carl L. *Freedom and Responsibility in the American Way of Life.* New York: Knopf, 1945.

Benokraitis, Nijole V., and Feagin, Joe R. *Affirmative Action and Equal Opportunity: Action, Inaction, Reaction.* Boulder: Westview Press, 1978.

Berns, Walter. *Freedom, Virtue, and the First Amendment.* Baton Rouge: Louisiana State University Press, 1957.

Berry, Mary Frances. *Military Necessity and Civil Rights Policy: Black Citizenship and the Constitution, 1861–1868.* Port Washington, N.Y.: Kennikat Press, 1977.

Blaustein, Albert P., and Ferguson, Clarence C. Jr. *Desegregation and the Law.* New Brunswick: Rutgers University Press, 1957.

Boles, Janet K. *The Politics of the Equal Rights Amendment: Conflict and the Decision Process.* New York: Longman Inc., 1979.

Brant, Irving. *The Bill of Rights: Its Origin and Meaning.* Indianapolis: Bobbs-Merrill, 1965.

Breckenridge, Adam Carlyle. *The Right to Privacy.* Lincoln: University of Nebraska Press, 1970.

Brenton, Myron. *The Privacy Invaders.* New York: Coward-McCann, 1964.

Brown, Everett Somerville. *Ratification of the Twenty-first Amendment to the Constitution of the United States: State Convention Records and Laws.* New York: Da Capo Press, 1970.

Cahn, Edmond, ed. *The Great Rights.* New York: Macmillan, 1963.

Carr, Robert K. *Federal Protection of Civil Rights: Quest for a Sword.* Ithaca: Cornell University Press, 1949.

Chaffee, Zechariah, Jr. *The Blessings of Liberty.* Philadelphia: J.B. Lippincott, 1956.

_____. *Documents on Fundamental Human Rights.* 3 vols. Cambridge: Harvard University Press, 1951.

_____. *Free Speech in the United States.* Cambridge: Harvard University Press, 1942.

_____. *How Human Rights Got into the Constitution.* Boston: Boston University Press, 1952.

Chase, Harold W. *Security and Liberty, the Problem of Native Communists, 1947–1955.* Garden City: Doubleday, 1955.

Commager, Henry S. *Freedom, Loyalty, Dissent.* New York: Oxford University Press, 1954.

Congressional Quarterly. *The Supreme Court and Individual Rights.* Washington: Congressional Quarterly, Inc., 1979.

Cook, Constance Ewing. *Nuclear Power and Legal Advocacy: The Environmentalists and the Courts.* Lexington, Mass.: Lexington Books, D.C. Heath, 1980.

Cook, Thomas I. *Democratic Rights Versus Communist Activity.* Garden City: Doubleday, 1954.

Corwin, Edward S. *Liberty Against Government.* Baton Rouge: Louisiana State University Press, 1948.

Cowles, Willard Bunce. *Treaties and Constitutional Law: Property Interferences and Due Process of Law.* Westport, Conn.: Greenwood Press, 1975.

Dilliard, Irving, ed. *The Spirit of Liberty: Papers and Addresses of Learned Hand.* 3rd ed. New York: Knopf, 1960.

Dixon, Robert G. *Democratic Representation: Reapportionment in Law and Politics.* New York: Oxford University Press, 1968.

Donner, Frank J. *The Age of Surveillance: The Aims and Methods of America's Political Intelligence System.* New York: Knopf, 1980.

Dorn, Edwin. *Rules and Racial Equality.* New Haven: Yale University Press, 1979.

Dorsen, Norman, ed. *The Rights of Americans: What They Are—What They Should Be.* New York: Vintage Books, 1971.

Dorsen, Norman, and Gillers, Stephen, eds. *None of Your Business: Government Secrecy in America.* New York: Penguin Books, 1975.

Douglas, William Orville. *Freedom of the Mind.* Garden City: Doubleday, 1964.

Elliff, John T. *The Reform of FBI Intelligence Operations.* Princeton: Princeton University Press, 1979.

Emerson, Thomas I. *The System of Freedom of Expression.* New York: Random House, 1970.

Ennis, Bruce, and Siegel, Loren. *The Rights of Mental Patients.* New York: Avon Books, 1973.

Engberg, Edward. *The Spy in the Corporate Structure and the Right to Privacy.* Cleveland: World Publishing Co., 1967.

Fairman, Charles, and Morrison, Stanley. *The Fourteenth Amendment and the Bill of Rights: The Incorporation Theory.* New York: Da Capo Press, 1970.

Fellman, David. *The Constitutional Right of Association.* Chicago: University of Chicago Press, 1963.

Fellman, David. *The Defendant's Rights Today.* Madison: The University of Wisconsin Press, 1976.

Flack, Horace Edgar. *The Adoption of the Fourteenth Amendment*. Gloucester, Mass.: P. Smith, 1965.

Freund, Paul. *Religion and the Public Schools*. Cambridge: Harvard University Press, 1965.

Friedland, Martin L. *Double Jeopardy*. Oxford: Clarendon Press, 1969.

Friedrich, Carl J. *Transcendent Justice: The Religious Dimensions of Constitutionalism*. Durham: Duke University Press, 1964.

Friendly, Alfred. *Crime and Publicity: The Impact of News and the Administration of Justice*. Millwood, N.Y.: Kraus Reprint Co., 1975.

Gellhorn, Walter. *Individual Freedom and Governmental Restraints*. Baton Rouge: Louisiana State University Press, 1956.

Gillette, William. *The Right to Vote: Politics and the Passage of the Fifteenth Amendment*. Baltimore: Johns Hopkins Press, 1965.

Gora, Joel M. *The Rights of Reporters*. New York: Avon Books, 1974.

Grimes, Alan P. *Democracy and the Amendments to the Constitution*. Lexington, Mass.: Lexington Books, 1978.

Griswold, Erwin N. *Search and Seizure: A Dilemma of the Supreme Court*. Lincoln: University of Nebraska Press, 1975.

Guthrie, William Cameron. *Lectures on the Fourteenth Article of Amendment to the Constitution of the United States*. New York: Da Capo Press, 1970.

Hachten, William A. *The Supreme Court on Freedom of the Press: Decisions and Dissents*. Ames: Iowa State University Press, 1968.

Hand, Learned. *The Bill of Rights*. New York: Atheneum, 1964.

Handlin, Oscar and Mary. *The Dimensions of Liberty*. Cambridge: Harvard University Press, 1961.

Hanson, Royce. *The Political Thicket: Reapportionment and Constitutional Democracy*. Englewood Cliffs: Prentice-Hall, 1966.

Harris, Robert J. *The Quest for Equality: The Constitution, Congress, and the Supreme Court*. Baton Rouge: Louisiana State University Press, 1960.

Hayden, Trudy. *Your Rights to Privacy: The Basic ACLU Guide for Your Rights to Privacy*. New York: Avon Books, 1980.

Heller, Francis Howard. *The Sixth Amendment to the Constitution of the United States: A Study in Constitutional Development*. New York: Greenwood Press, 1969.

Hemmer, Joseph J. *Free Speech*. Millbrae, Calif.: Scarecrow, 1979.

Hentoff, Nat. *The First Freedom: The Tumultuous History of Free Speech in America*. New York: Delacorte, 1980.

Heumann, Milton. *Plea Bargaining: The Experiences of Prosecutors, Judges, and Defense Attorneys*. Chicago: University of Chicago Press, 1978.

Howe, Mark De Wolfe. *Garden and the Wilderness: Religion and Government in American Constitutional History*. Chicago: University of Chicago Press, 1965.

Hudson, Edward. *Freedom of Speech and Press in America*. Washington: Public Affairs Press, 1963.

Humphrey, Hubert H., ed. *School Desegregation: Documents and Commentaries*. New York: Thomas Crowell, 1964.

Kalven, Harry. *The Negro and the First Amendment*. Columbus: Ohio State University Press, 1965.

Kauper, Paul G. *Religion and the Constitution*. Baton Rouge: Louisiana State University Press, 1964.

Konvitz, Milton R. *Fundamental Liberties of a Free People: Religion, Speech, Press, Assembly*. Ithaca: Cornell University Press, 1957.

————. *A Century of Civil Rights*. New York: Columbia University Press, 1967.

————. *Religious Liberty and Conscience: A Constitutional Inquiry*. New York: Viking Press, 1968.

Kurland, Philip B. *Religion and the Law*. Chicago: Aldine Publishing Company, 1962.

Landynski, Jacob W. *Searches and Seizures and the Supreme Court*. Baltimore: Johns Hopkins University Press, 1966.

Lasson, Nelson Bernard. *The History and Development of the Fourth Amendment to the United States Constitution*. New York: Da Capo Press, 1970.

Lasswell, Harold D. *National Security and Individual Freedom*. New York: McGraw-Hill, 1950.

Law, Sylvia. *The Rights of the Poor*. New York: Avon Books, 1974.

Lester, Richard A. *Reasoning About Discrimination: The Analysis of Professional and Executive Work in Federal Antibias Programs*. Princeton: Princeton University Press, 1980.

Levine, Alan H.; Carey, Eve; and Divoky, Diane. *The Rights of Students*. New York: Avon Books, 1973.

Levitan, Sar A.; Johnston, William B.; and Taggart, Robert. *Minorities in the United States*. Washington: Public Affairs Press, 1976.

Levy, Leonard, ed. *Freedom of the Press from Zenger to Jefferson: Early American Libertarian Theories*. Indianapolis: Bobbs-Merrill Co., 1966.

Levy, Leonard. *Jefferson and Civil Liberties: The Darker Side*. Cambridge: Harvard University Press, 1963.

————. *Legacy of Suppression, Freedom of Speech and Press in Early American History*. Cambridge: Harvard University Press, 1960.

————. *Origins of the Fifth Amendment: The Right Against Self-Incrimination*. New York: Oxford University Press, 1968.

Lewis, Anthony. *Gideon's Trumpet*. New York: Random House, 1960.

Lien, Arnold Johnson. *Concurring Opinion: the Privileges or Immunities Clause of the Fourteenth Amendment*. Westport, Conn.: Greenwood Press, 1975.

Lofton, John. *The Press as Guardian of the First Amendment*. Columbia: University of South Carolina Press, 1980.

Longaker, Richard P. *The Presidency and Civil Liberties*. Ithaca: Cornell University Press, 1962.

Manwaring, David P. *Render unto Caesar, the Flag-Salute Controversy*. Chicago: University of Chicago Press, 1962.

Martin, John Frederick. *Civil Rights and the Crisis of Liberalism: The Democratic Party 1945-1976*. Boulder, Col.: Westview Press, 1979.

Mathews, John Mabry. *Legislative and Judicial History of the Fifteenth Amendment*. New York: Da Capo Press, 1971.

McKay, Robert. *Reapportionment: The Law and Politics of Equal Representation*. New York: Twentieth Century Fund, 1965.

Meiklejohn, Alexander. *Free Speech in Relation to Self-Government*. Port Washington, N.Y.: Kennikat Press, 1971.

————. *Political Freedom: The Constitutional Powers of the People*. New York: Harper and Row, 1960.

Meltsner, M. *Cruel and Unusual: the Supreme Court and Capital Punishment*. New York: Morrow, 1973.

Mendelson, Wallace. *Discrimination, Based on the Report of the United States Commission on Civil Rights.* Englewood Cliffs: Prentice-Hall, 1962.
Meyer, Hermine Herta. *The History and Meaning of the Fourteenth Amendment: Judicial Erosion of the Constitution Through the Misuse of the Fourteenth Amendment.* New York: Vantage Press, 1977.
Miller, Leonard G. *Double Jeopardy and The Federal System.* Chicago: University of Chicago Press, 1968.
Milner, Neal A. *The Court and Local Law Enforcement: the Impact of Miranda.* Beverly Hills, California: Sage Publications, 1971.
Morgan, Richard E. *Domestic Intelligence: Monitoring Dissent in America.* Austin: University of Texas Press, 1980.
_____. *The Politics of Religious Conflict: Church and State in America.* 2nd ed. Washington: University Press of America, 1980.
_____. *The Supreme Court and Religion.* New York: Free Press, 1972.
Murphy, Paul L. *The Meaning of Freedom of Speech: First Amendment Freedoms from Wilson to FDR.* Westport: Greenwood, 1973.
Murphy, Walter F. *Wiretapping on Trial: A Case Study in the Judicial Process.* New York: Random House, 1965.
Nelson, Harold L., ed. *Freedom of the Press from Hamilton to the Warren Court.* Indianapolis: Bobbs-Merrill, 1967.
Newfield, J. *Cruel and Unusual Justice.* New York: Holt, Rinehart and Winston, 1974.
O'Brian, John L. *National Security and Individual Freedom.* Cambridge: Harvard University Press, 1955.
O'Brien, David M. *Privacy, Law, and Public Policy.* New York: Praeger Publishers, 1979.
O'Connor, Karen. *Women's Organizations' Use of the Courts.* Lexington, Ma.: Lexington Books, 1980.
Orfield, Gary. *Must We Bus? Segregated Schools and National Policy.* Washington: The Brookings Institution, 1978.
O'Rourke, Timothy G. *The Impact of Reapportionment.* New Brunswick, N.J.: Transaction Books, 1980.
Peltason, Jack W. *Fifty-Eight Lonely Men, Southern Federal Judges and School Desegregation.* New York: Harcourt, Brace and World, 1961.
Perry, Richard L. *Sources of Our Liberties.* Chicago: American Bar Foundation, 1959.
Pfeffer, Leo. *Church, State, and Freedom.* Boston: Beacon Press, 1967.
_____. *Church and State in the United States.* New York: Harper & Row, 1964.
_____. *The Liberties of an American.* Boston: Beacon Press, 1956.
Pipel, Harriet E. *Obscenity and the Constitution.* New York: R.R. Bowker, 1973.
Pound, Roscoe. *The Development of Constitutional Guarantees of Liberty.* New Haven: Yale University Press, 1957.
Prettyman, Barrett, Jr. *Death and the Supreme Court.* New York: Harcourt, Brace and World, 1961.
Pritchett, C. Herman. *Civil Liberties and the Vinson Court.* Chicago: University of Chicago Press, 1954.
_____. *The Political Offender and the Warren Court.* Boston: Boston University Press, 1958.
Rankin, Robert S., and Dallmayr, Winifred R. *Freedom and Emergency Powers in the Cold War.* New York: Appleton-Century-Crofts, 1964.
Rivkin, Robert S. *The Rights of Servicemen.* New York: Avon Books, 1972.

Roche, John T. *Courts and Rights, The American Judiciary in Action.* New York: Random House, 1961.

Roettinger, Ruth L. *The Supreme Court and State Police Power.* Washington: Public Affairs Press, 1957.

Rogge, O. John. *The First and the Fifth* [Amendments]. New York: Da Capo Press, 1971.

Rosengart, Oliver. *The Rights of Suspects.* New York: Avon Books, 1974.

Ross, Susan C. *The Rights of Women.* New York: Avon Books, 1973.

Rudovsky, David. *The Rights of Prisoners.* New York: Avon Books, 1973.

Rutland, Robert A. *The Birth of the Bill of Rights, 1776–1791.* Chapel Hill: University of North Carolina Press, 1955.

Schlesinger, Steven R. *Exclusionary Injustice: The Problem of Illegally Obtained Evidence.* New York: Marcel Dekker, 1977.

Schwartz, Bernard, ed. *The Fourteenth Amendment: Centennial Volume.* New York: New York University Press, 1970.

Schwartz, Bernard. *The Great Rights of Mankind: A History of the American Bill of Rights.* New York: Oxford University Press, 1977.

Schwartz, Bernard, ed. *Statutary History of the United States: Civil Rights.* 2 vols. New York: Chelsea House, 1970.

Shapiro, Martin. *Freedom of Speech: the Supreme Court and Judicial Review.* Englewood Cliffs: Prentice-Hall, 1966.

_____. *The Pentagon Papers and the Courts: A Study in Foreign Policy Making and Freedom of the Press.* San Francisco: Chandler Publishing Co., 1972.

Sigler, Jay A. *Double Jeopardy: The Development of a Legal and Social Policy.* Ithaca, N.Y.: Cornell University Press, 1969.

Sindler, Allan P. *Bakke, Defunis, and Minority Admissions: The Quest for Equal Opportunity.* New York: Longman Inc., 1978.

Stephens, Otis H. *The Supreme Court and Confessions of Guilt.* Nashville: University of Tennessee Press, 1973.

Stouffer, Samuel A. *Communism, Conformity, and Civil Liberties.* Garden City, N.Y.: Doubleday, 1955.

Taper, Bernard. *Gomillion v. Lightfoot, the Tuskegee Gerrymander Case.* New York: McGraw-Hill, 1962.

Taylor, Telford. *Two Studies in Constitutional Interpretations: Search, Seizure, and Surveillance, and Fair Trial and Free Press.* Columbus: Ohio State University Press, 1969.

Ten Broek, Jacobus. *Equal Under Law* [*Anti-Slavery Origins of the Fourteenth Amendment*]. New York: Collier Books, 1965.

Theoharis, Athan. *Spying on Americans: Political Surveillance from Hoover to the Huston Plan.* Philadelphia: Temple University Press, 1978.

Van Gerpen, Maurice. *Privileged Communication and the Press: The Citizen's Right to Know versus the Law's Right to Confidential News Source Evidence.* Westport, Conn.: Greenwood Press, 1979.

Vose, Clement E. *Caucasians Only: The Supreme Court, the NAACP, and the Restrictive Covenant Cases.* Berkeley: University of California Press, 1959.

Warren, Earl. *The Bill of Rights and the Military.* New York: University Law Center, 1962.

Warsoff, Louis A. *Equality and the Law.* Westport, Conn.: Greenwood, 1975.

Wasby, Stephen L.; D'Amato, Anthony A.; and Metrailer, Rosemary. *Desegregation from Brown to Alexander: An Exploration of Supreme Court Strategies*. Carbondale: Southern Illinois University Press, 1977.

Way, H. Frank. *Liberty in Balance: Current Issues in Civil Liberties*. 5th ed. New York: McGraw-Hill, 1981.

Westin, Alan. *Privacy and Freedom*. New York: Atheneum, 1967.

Wise, David. *The American Police State*. New York: Random House, 1976.

Zangrando, Robert L. *The NAACP Crusade Against Lynching, 1909–1950*. Philadelphia: Temple University Press, 1980.

LAW AND SOCIETY

Alcock, Antony E.; Taylor, Brian K.; and Welton, John M. *The Future of Cultural Minorities*. New York: St. Martin's Press, 1979.

Alix, Ernest Kahlar. *Ransom Kidnapping in America, 1874–1974*. Carbondale: Southern Illinois University Press, 1978.

Bayley, David. *Forces of Order: Police Behavior in Japan and in the United States*. Berkeley: University of California Press, 1976.

Berkman, Ronald. *Opening the Gates: The Rise of the Prisoners' Movement*. Lexington, Mass.: Lexington Books, 1979.

Bohannan, Paul, ed. *Law and Warfare*. Garden City, N.Y.: Natural History Press, 1967.

Bonsignore, John J.; Katsh, Ethan; d'Errico, Peter; Pipkin, Ronald M.; Arons, Stephen; and Rifkin, Janet. *Before the Law: An Introduction to the Legal Process*. 2d ed. Boston: Houghton Mifflin, 1979.

Braithwaite, John. *Inequality, Crime and Public Policy*. Boston: Routledge and Kegan Paul, 1979.

Bromberg, Walter. *The Uses of Psychiatry in the Law: A Clinical View of Forensic Psychiatry*. Westport, Conn.: Greenwood, 1979.

Burkhardt, Kathryn. *Women in Prison*. Garden City, N.Y.: Doubleday, 1973.

Burt, Robert A. *Taking Care of Strangers: The Rule of Law in Doctor-Patient Relations*. New York: The Free Press, 1979.

Cain, Maureen, and Hunt, Alan. *Marx and Engels on Law*. New York: Academic Press, 1979.

Chambliss, William, and Seidman, Robert. *Law, Order and Power*. Reading, Mass.: Addison-Wesley, 1971.

Cleaver, Eldridge. *Soul On Ice*. New York: McGraw-Hill, 1968.

Cohen, Morris L.; Ronen, Naomi; and Stepan, Jan; comps. *Law and Science*. Cambridge, Ma.: The MIT Press, 1980.

Coser, Lewis. *The Functions of Social Conflict*. New York: The Free Press, 1956.

Davis, Karl. *Discretionary Justice*. Baton Rouge: Louisiana State University Press, 1969.

Ehrlich, Eugen. *Fundamental Principles of the Sociology of Law*. Translated by W. Moll. New York: Russell and Russell, 1962.

Erikson, Kai T. *Wayward Puritans: A Study in the Sociology of Deviance*. New York: John Wiley and Sons, 1966.

Feild, Hubert S., and Bienen, Leigh B. *Jurors and Rape: A Study in Psychology and Law*. Lexington, Mass.: Lexington Books, 1980.

Forsyth. Walter, *History of Trial by Jury*. New York: Burt Franklin, 1971.

Foucault, Michel. *The Birth of the Prison*. New York: Pantheon, 1978.

Foust, Cleon H., and Webster, Robert D. *An Anatomy of Criminal Justice*. Lexington, Mass.: Lexington Books, 1980.

Gardiner, John A., ed. *Public Law and Public Policy*. New York: Praeger Publishers, 1977.

Geis, Gilbert, and Stotland, Ezra. *White-Collar Crime: Theory and Research*. Beverly Hills: Sage Publications, 1980.

Goldstein, Paul J. *Prostitution and Drugs*. Lexington, Mass.: Lexington Books, 1979.

Gould, David J. *Law and the Administrative Process: Analytic Frameworks for Understanding Public Policymaking*. Washington: University Press of America, 1979.

Gregory, Charles O., and Katz, Harold A. *Labor and the Law*. 3rd ed. New York: W. W. Norton, 1979.

Grilliot, Harold J. *Introduction to Law and the Legal System*. 2d ed. Boston: Houghton Mifflin, 1979.

Grossman, Joel B., and Grossman, Mary H., eds. *Law and Change in Modern America*. Pacific Palisades, Calif.: Goodyear Publishing, 1971.

Gulliver, P.H., ed. *Cross-Examinations: Essays in Memory of Max Gluckman*. Leiden, The Netherlands: E.J. Brill, 1978.

Gulliver, P.H. *Disputes and Negotiations: A Cross-Cultural Perspective*. New York: Academic Press, Inc. 1979.

Gurr, Ted Robert. *Violence in America: Historical and Comparative Perspectives*. New York: Bantam Books, 1970.

Hartzler, H. Richard, and Allan, Harry. *An Introduction to Law*. Glenview, Ill.: Scott, Foresman, 1969.

Harris, John. *Violence and Responsibility*. Boston: Routledge and Kegan Paul, 1980.

Hirsch, Werner Z. *Law and Economics: An Introductory Analysis*. New York: Academic Press, 1979.

Hudson, Joe, and Galaway, Burt. eds. *Victims, Offenders, and Alternative Sanctions*. Lexington, Mass.: Lexington Books, 1980.

Kalven, Harry, Jr., and Zeisel, Hans. *The American Jury*. Boston: Little, Brown, 1966.

Karlen, Delmar. *The Citizen in Court*. New York: Holt, Rinehart and Winston, 1964.

Kirchheimer, Otto. *Political Justice*. Princeton: Princeton University Press, 1961.

Kolasa, Blair J., and Meyer, Bernadine. *Legal Systems*. Englewood Cliffs: Prentice-Hall, 1978.

Levine, James P.; Musheno, Michael C.; and Palumbo, Dennis J. *Criminal Justice: A Public Policy Approach*. New York: Harcourt, Brace and Jovanovich, 1980.

Lieberman, Jethro K. *The Litigious Society*. New York: Basic Books Inc., 1980.

Llewellyn, Karl, and Hoebel, E. Adamson. *The Cheyenne Way*. Norman: University of Oklahoma Press, 1941.

Macneil, Iran R. *The New Social Contract: An Inquiry into Modern Contractual Relations*. New Haven: Yale University Press, 1980.

Maine, Henry. *Ancient Law*. London: Oxford University Press, 1931.

Malinchak, Alan A. *Crime and Gerontology*. Englewood Cliffs: Prentice-Hall, Inc., 1980.

Menninger, Karl. *The Crime of Punishment*. New York: Viking Press, 1968.

Merryman, John Henry; Clark, David S.; and Friedman, Lawrence M. *Law and Social Change in Mediterranean Europe and Latin America: A Handbook of Legal and Social Indicators for Comparative Study*. Dobbs Ferry, N.Y.: Oceana Publications, Inc., 1980.

Morris, Norville. *The Future of Imprisonment.* Chicago: University of Chicago Press, 1977.

Nader, Laura, ed. *Law in Culture and Society.* Chicago: Aldine, 1969.

Pound, Roscoe. *Social Control Through Law.* New Haven: Yale University Press, 1942.

Quinney, Richard. *Critique of Legal Order.* Boston: Little, Brown, 1974.

———. *Class, State and Crime.* New York: McKay, 1977.

Reiss, Albert. *The Police and the Public.* New Haven: Yale University Press, 1971.

Robbins, Ira P. *Comparative Postconviction Remedies.* Lexington, Mass.: Lexington Books, 1980.

Saks, Michael. *Jury Verdict: The Role of Group Size and Social Decision-Rule.* Lexington, Mass.: Lexington Books, 1977.

Schichor, David, and Kelly, Delos H., eds. *Critical Issues in Juvenile Delinquency.* Lexington, Mass.: Lexington Books, 1980.

Schur, Edwin. *Law and Society.* New York: Random House, 1968.

Schwitzgebel, Robert L., and Schwitzgebel, R. Kirland. *Law and Psychological Practice.* New York: John Wiley & Sons, 1980.

Siegan, Bernard H. *Regulation, Economics, and the Law.* Lexington, Mass.: Lexington Books, 1979.

Simon, Rita James, ed. *The Sociology of Law: Interdisciplinary Readings.* San Francisco: Chandler Publishing, 1968.

Skolnick, Jerome. *Justice without Trial: Law Enforcement in a Democratic Society.* New York: John Wiley, 1966.

Summers, Robert. *Law: Its Nature, Functions and Limits.* Englewood Cliffs: Prentice-Hall, 1972.

Szasz, Thomas. *Law, Liberty and Psychiatry.* New York: Macmillan, 1963.

———. *Psychiatric Justice.* New York: Collier Books, 1965.

Thornes, Barbara, and Collard, Jean. *Who Divorces?* Boston: Routledge and Kegan Paul, 1979.

Tönnies, Ferdinand. *Community and Society.* Edited and translated by Charles P. Loomis. New York: Harper and Row, 1963.

Walker, Samuel. *Popular Justice: A History of American Criminal Justice.* New York: Oxford University Press, 1980.

Weber, Max. *On Law in Economy and Society.* Translated with introduction by Max Rheinstein et al. Cambridge: Harvard University Press, 1954.

Wechsler, Henry, ed. *Minimum Drinking Age Laws: An Evaluation.* Lexington, Mass.: Lexington Books, 1980.

Weinberg, Lee S., and Weinberg, Judith W. *Law and Society: An Interdisciplinary Introduction.* Washington: University Press of America, 1980.

Westley, William A. *Violence and the Police.* Cambridge: MIT Press, 1971.

Wilson, James Q. *Varieties of Police Behavior.* Cambridge: Harvard University Press, 1968.

Wright, Eric Olin. *The Politics of Punishment.* New York: Harper Colophon Books, Harper and Row, 1973.

Yarmey, A. Daniel. *The Psychology of Eyewitness Testimony.* New York: The Free Press, 1979.

LEGAL PROFESSION

Auerbach, Jerome. *Unequal Justice.* New York: Oxford University Press, 1976.

Black, Jonathan, ed. *Radical Lawyers.* New York: Avon Books, 1971.

Bloomfield, Maxwell. *American Lawyers in a Changing Society, 1776–1876.* Cambridge: Harvard University Press, 1976.

Carlin, Jerome E. *Lawyers on Their Own.* New Brunswick: Rutgers University Press, 1962.

Casper, Jonathan D. *Lawyers Before the Warren Court: Civil Liberties and Civil Rights, 1957–1966.* Urbana: University of Illinois Press, 1972.

Eisenstein, James. *Counsel for the United States: U.S. Attorney in the Political and Legal System.* Baltimore: John Hopkins University Press, 1978.

Ginger, Ann Fagan. *The Relevant Lawyers.* New York: Simon and Schuster, 1972.

Goulden, Joseph. *The Super-Lawyers.* New York: Weybright & Talley, 1971.

Grossman, Joel B. *Lawyers and Judges: The ABA and the Politics of Judicial Selection.* New York: John Wiley and Sons, 1965.

Handler, Joel. *The Lawyer and his Community.* Madison: University of Wisconsin Press, 1967.

Hurst, James Willard. *The Growth of American Law.* Boston: Little, Brown, 1950.

Lefcourt, Robert. *Law Against the People.* New York: Vintage Books, 1971.

Mayer, Martin. *The Lawyers.* New York: Dell Publishing, 1968.

Medcalf. Linda. *Law and Identity: Lawyers, Native Americans, and Legal Practice.* Beverly Hills: Sage Publications, 1978.

Melone, Albert P. *Lawyers, Public Policy and Interest Group Politics.* Washington: University Press of America, 1977.

Pound, Roscoe. *The Lawyer from Antiquity to Modern Times.* St. Paul: West Publishing, 1953.

Rosenthal, Douglas. *Lawyer and Client: Who's in Charge?* New Brunswick, N.Y.: Transaction Books, 1974.

Shaffer, Thomas and Redmount, Robert. *Lawyers, Law Students and People.* Indianapolis: Sheppard's, 1977.

Smigel, Erwin O. *The Wall Street Lawyer.* New York: The Free Press, 1964.

Stumpf, Harry P. *Community Politics and Legal Services.* Beverly Hills: Sage Publications, 1975.

Twiss, Benjamin. *Lawyers and the Constitution.* Princeton: Princeton University Press, 1942.

Warren, Charles. *A History of the American Bar.* Boston: Little, Brown, 1911.

Wice, Paul B. *Criminal Lawyer: An Endangered Species.* Beverly Hills: Sage Publications, 1978.

Wood, Arthur Lewis. *Criminal Lawyer.* New Haven: College & University Press, 1967.

Index